The Quiet Achiever

Tiny habits to have impact at work without pretending to be an extrovert

Tim Yeo

TQA
Scan to listen

*Just because I'm quiet doesn't
mean I have nothing to say.*

Dedication

To the women in my life: Angélique, my love; Bobbie, my rock; and Mama, my strength. My heart is you.

Contents

Chapter 1

Introduction

I grew up and started my career in Singapore, a city-state in Southeast Asia (where, you might be surprised to know, English is our first language).

Where I am from, we do not talk to random strangers on the street. Most of us would rather be reading a book or magazine or staring at our phones—you know, like most people do.

Years later I moved to Australia, a Western society, for work, and I was surprised by how much strangers here seemed to love small talk. Small talk happened everywhere: I could be in a queue waiting for a bus, tram, or train, standing in the checkout line waiting to pay, walking down the aisle of a grocery store, standing at a bar waiting to get a drink, or even waiting to use the toilet! Somehow, small talk would creep up on me when I least expected it.

I had to learn how to talk about the weather and ask people how they were doing, what their plans were for the weekend, etc. In the beginning, when people asked me how I was, I would give them a genuine answer. But I quickly came to realise I was probably oversharing and that they were not really that interested in my response (they were just saying hi).

And it was not just small talk I found difficult as I progressed through my career.

For years, I struggled to manage my introversion. I received feedback from my bosses like "you should speak up more in meetings," but I did not know how. I found myself in rooms full of people with strong opinions and loud voices, and I did not know how to be heard.

I gave away opportunities to present my work because I struggled with public speaking, only to resent myself and feel jealous as I watched others get all the credit even though they had done none of the work. When I did say yes, I would have sleepless nights beforehand. When presenting, I was so nervous my voice would shake, my hands would tremble, and my mind would go blank. Afterwards, I could not even remember what I'd said or why I'd said it, even though I had prepared and rehearsed everything beforehand.

I'd say "yes" to unreasonable requests, even though I thought *no*, just to avoid having a difficult conversation. I felt like a doormat, getting walked over by anyone and everyone just because I could not say what I wanted.

I'd go to networking events, only to stand in the corner of the room or stick to the few people I knew. I was nervous about approaching strangers to say hi. I'd hide in the bathroom when it all felt like too much. I wondered how others did it; they made it look so easy. I wondered why I'd come in the first place. I wanted to leave as soon as I arrived.

At interviews, "tell me about yourself" were my four least favourite words. I'd speak for too long and end up sharing unimportant details. I could not stop talking even when I noticed the interviewers had lost interest. I used "we" instead of "I" when talking about my accomplishments at work. I did not enjoy singing my own praises because it would shine a spotlight on me and the glare was uncomfortable.

I watched as the louder voices got the recognition and the promotions. But even though these louder voices seemed to say the most, they did not always have the most to say.

Susan Cain said it best in her book *Quiet* :[1] "We live in a world where the extrovert ideal is desired." At the time, this was the picture of what a leader looked like to me:

- A leader commands the centre of attention

- A leader is outgoing, talkative, and dominant

- A leader is able to deliver charismatic speeches and rally large audiences at the drop of a hat

In essence, I thought a leader was an extrovert. Back then, I wished that I was more extroverted. So for a long time, I pretended. I thought that if I wanted to be a leader, I needed to be extroverted all the time. I thought that if I pretended hard enough, I could be just like the leaders I looked up to. And for a while, it worked.

But I was exhausted. Every day, I felt like I was putting on a mask and pretending to be someone else. With each passing day, that mask grew heavier and heavier, until one day, I could not pick up that mask and put it on anymore. I was tired of pretending to be someone I was not. I kept thinking: *What's wrong with me? Maybe I'm just not good enough. Maybe I should just give up.*

But there was another voice inside of me that refused to be silenced. That voice was stubborn, and it told me there had to be another way.

So I went into sponge mode. I read and learned as widely as I could about introversion, self-help, and quiet leadership. I absorbed everything I read and grew hungry for more. From networking to public speaking, improv to influence, small talk to crucial conversations, tiny habits to office politics to fearless negotiation—I read about it all.

While much of what I read was inspiring and motivating, there remained one problem: I did not know how to apply what I learned. While most of what I read made me feel good, very few books or articles included concrete actions I could take to address my problems the very next day.

So I started doing things my own way.

I started with small, low-stakes actions. I performed best in 1:1 relationships, so I built more 1:1 relationships at work. I organised regular coffee catchups with senior leaders from work so they could hear my ideas early; I listened to their feedback and influenced their thinking from the very start.

I walked around the office for the first 30 minutes of every workday engaging with colleagues from other departments, asking how their work was going and how I could help.

I facilitated workshops where my superiors and peers followed my lead. I recorded short videos of myself presenting my work and shared them with our teams around the world, giving me the chance to speak up for my work instead of someone else doing it on my behalf.

I practised presentations twice as hard as others so that my words would seem natural and effortless. I networked online for at least 15 minutes every single day instead of going to networking events with strangers once a month. I pushed back on unreasonable requests and rehearsed difficult conversations beforehand so I would stay on track.

And it worked. I ran workshops so well that executives in my company invited me to organise and facilitate executive workshops. Colleagues who I had never met before would come up to me and say, "Hey! You're Tim. I saw your video; you designed that feature in the last release. Nice work!" My actions showed I was a team player.

I delivered keynote speeches at international conferences in front of hundreds of people. I had difficult conversations with peers. I made small talk so often it became second nature. I networked online and met many of my career heroes, people I once only knew through their books.

I'd finally arrived.

My epiphany was realising there is more than one path to success, and my path is simply different.

The self-doubt and low self-esteem that I had felt for being terrible at public speaking, being awkward at small talk, and saying "yes" when I thought *no*—all that negativity had come from comparing myself to others and thinking about how easy other people made it look when they were doing the same thing as me. Comparison was my recipe for misery.

My new path to success is the sum of tiny habits, done well, accumulated over time. Same success, different path. I do not need to be loud; I can be quiet and still have impact and influence. I can be me and still be successful. I am enough.

This book is a collection of the tiny habits that I developed, practised, and helped others learn over my years of coaching and workshops. These habits helped me and others have an impact and influence at work while remaining true to our authentic selves.

You should know: This personal growth will stretch you. It may feel uncomfortable trying something new for the first time. You will make mistakes. Do not give up; try again. You will soon learn to thicken your skin without hardening your heart.

If all this sounds like a lot of work, it is. These tiny habits are skills you need to practise. Reading about them in this book is a great first step. But no change will happen until you try it out in real life. I know this is true because I've coached and run courses with hundreds of quiet achievers. The ones who practise win.

Just because we are quiet does not mean we have nothing to say. I wrote this book for the quiet achievers with loud minds who, like me, want to learn "how to people." Being quiet is not a flaw; it's a superpower. And I hope these tiny habits will help your superpower shine.

Who is this book for?

This book is for:

- Quiet achievers and introverts—people like me—who want to have impact at work without pretending to be extroverts

- People who are not quite sure if they identify as introverts, extroverts, or ambiverts (yet) but still want to learn "how to people"

- Ambiverts and extroverts who want to learn how to work better with their quiet peers

- Managers of teams that skew quiet and who want to learn how to get the best out of their people

What does it feel like to be a quiet achiever?

- You do not like the glare of the spotlight or other people's attention on you. There is no nightmare worse than being surprised at a company event when your boss suddenly says, "Would you like to say a few words?" and having everyone stare at you while you don't know what to say

- You use "we" and talk about "our team effort" even though, in reality, all/most of the work was done by you—because you do not want to stand out

- Speaking up on the spot does not come naturally to you; you need more time to process your thinking before you are ready to speak. If a question is asked in a meeting, you are not ready to speak and need time to process first

- You like social interactions, but because they drain your energy, you want them in small doses

- You can be the chattiest person in a group of people you know well, but bring even one total stranger into the group and you go quiet

- You are comfortable sharing your thoughts openly with groups of up to six people, but no bigger

- Working in open-plan offices is distracting and over-stimulating. You often wear headphones in order to focus and use it as a signal to tell others you prefer not to be disturbed

- On your first day at work or when it's your first time working with a new team, you always get nervous and dread introducing yourself

- You go quiet if there are louder people in the room

- A quiet weekend with books, movies, and painting energises you more than parties socialising with strangers

- Standing up and presenting work in front of people makes you anxious. You prepare and rehearse, but when it's showtime, you still feel nervous

- You find it hard to get other people's attention, whether it is coworkers in a meeting or waiters at a restaurant

Introversion and extroversion are not absolute states of behaviour. How we behave depends on context, environment, and the people that are around us at the time. No one is truly an introvert or extrovert all of the time; our identity depends on how we behave most of the time.

You might notice that I use the phrase "quiet achiever" rather than "introvert" in this book. I do this intentionally. I did not really understand introversion until I read Susan Cain's book *Quiet* in 2012. When I did, I embraced the word "introvert" fully.

But society at large desires the extrovert ideal. This has a strong influence on all of us. I have coached quiet achievers who did not embrace the word "introvert" because they saw introversion as a weakness to get rid of. They wanted to live society's version of what the ideal person looks like and saw their introversion as a flaw to be fixed.

So I have chosen the phrase "quiet achiever" deliberately. It speaks to our drive and ambition. It also speaks to the way we achieve: Not loudly, but quietly. It has all the accuracy for readers to self-identify as the target audience of this book without the loaded expectations society brings to the word "introvert." Life is a journey; self-discovery takes time. Take all the time you need.

Even then, maybe you do not want to be pigeonholed into one label. Perhaps you are many things to many people and see both "introvert" and "quiet achiever" as limiting. That is cool with me. If you face similar challenges at work, if you exhibit similar behaviours and these tiny habits work for you, then this book is for you too.

How to read this book

I designed this book to be read in two different ways.

Got a problem right now? Jump straight to the chapter which talks about the issue you are struggling with at the moment. Read it. Learn the tiny habit. Practise and apply it to your situation right now.

Remember, trying something new will stretch you. If you do not try, you will never know. It may feel uncomfortable; that's what growth feels like. If you feel like giving up, ask yourself: *Do I really want to go back to being the person I was before?*

Got time? You can probably read this whole book in less than two hours.

As you read, highlight meaningful words. Make notes. Place bookmarks. Dog-ear the pages. Leave a trail so it is easy to revisit the book the next time you read it. Memories fade. You might be surprised how the words resonate differently on subsequent reads and after new life experiences. This book was once mine, but it is yours now. Make it your own. There is no greater crime than a read book with zero markings in it.

Think back to a time you faced a similar challenge. Immerse yourself in that moment; really take yourself back. You did not know this tiny habit back then, but you do now. If you could go back in time, what would you do differently?

There is only one key to success with this book, and that is practise. Reading the book is great. Imagining how you will put these tiny habits into action is even better. But no change will happen until you practice these habits in real life.

Try; give it a go. Start with low stakes. Practise alone (I do). Have your most glorious moments of failure in private so that nobody will ever see. Inject your personality into these tiny habits to make them your own. Most importantly, practise, practise, practise these tiny habits. Some will come quickly. Others will take time. Repeat them until they come naturally to you.

These habits are tried and tested by me and others I've coached. They can help you too. Just keep practising.

Chapter 2

Introducing yourself

No two phrases send a shiver down my spine and make me want to shrink back into my shell more than:

> Tell me about yourself.

and

> Let's go around the room and introduce ourselves.

I'd hear these words on the first day of joining a new company, at the start of a job interview, or when meeting a new team of people. And I dreaded them.

What should I say? How much detail is too much detail? Quick, think of something funny! What is one interesting thing about me that I can share? Gosh, why can't I think of one, just one, thing right now? Oh no...it is my turn soon. Why do I feel more and more nervous the closer it is to my turn? How is it that everyone else seems to make it look so easy? Why do I always think of the right thing to say two minutes after my turn?

I was prepared when it came to the work itself. On my first day, I'd have reasons why I was excited to join this team or start this work. At interviews, I'd have notable work examples from my previous roles. In meetings, I'd have presentation slides for every item on the agenda.

But I was never prepared for the introductions. They were a social ritual that predictably happened every time at the start of something new. Yet introductions caught me off guard every time.

Why is it important to introduce yourself well?

Introductions are important because if you start well, you end well. Starting well gives you the confidence to keep going strong and leave a positive first impression.

It is also the part of social interactions that you are most in control of. You have less control over the rest of the session because others are involved. But you're firmly in the driver's seat when introducing yourself.

What makes a good introduction

A good introduction:

- Is memorable

- Lets them know your name

- Shares just enough information to get the conversation started

- Lets them know how to contact you

- Piques their interest

- Lets them decide where to explore next

Introductions can be used:

- When meeting in person or virtually

- In both synchronous (live, real time) and asynchronous (not live, at a time you decide) communication[2]

- With people you know and/or people you are meeting for the first time

Bad introductions go on for far too long; you do not know how to stop, even when you notice the audience has clearly lost interest. Bad introductions are messy and incoherent. You jump from one random fact to another. You keep talking, but you are not even sure why you are sharing the things you are saying. You are not prepared, and you improvise even though thinking on the spot is not your strength.

Introductions are the one part of social interactions that happen over and over again. So it makes sense to practise and get good at them. Here is how you do it.

Introductions come in three sizes

Introductions are not one-size-fits-all. Contexts change, and so you need introductions of different sizes to suit the situation, environment, and audience.

All introductions are monologues, and they come in three sizes which suit a majority of contexts:

1. **Small**: Said in one breath, in 10 seconds or less, and in 20 words or less

2. **Medium**: Said in one to three minutes (the norm is one minute)

3. **Large**: Said in five minutes or less

Small introductions

A small introduction is something you can say in one breath: In 10 seconds or less, in 20 words or less.

Audiences and scenarios where small introductions are useful include:

- **Networking**: Meeting new people in noisy environments for short periods of time

- **Meetings**: A group of more than five people taking turns going around the room to briefly introduce themselves before the session begins

A small introduction uses a combination of the following variables:

- Your Name

- Target audience

- Need, benefit, or opportunity you satisfy

- Differentiator

- Something people want or need

- Negative consequence you prevent

- A problem you can fix

Fill these variables into one of the following templates:[3]

- I'm [your name]. I help [target audience] do [statement of need] and [statement of benefit]

- I'm [your name]. I help [target audience] do [statement of need or opportunity] through [differentiator]

- I'm [your name]. I help [target audience] achieve [something they want] without [negative consequence]

- I'm [your name]. I [transform/translate/convert a problem] into [something aspirational]

- I'm [your name]. I help [target audience] [fix their problem]

For example:

- I'm Tim. I walk antisocial dogs in groups of three or fewer and return them tired, happy, and safe

- I'm Tim. I help small business owners build websites without spending a lot of money

- I'm Tim. I help introverts have impact and influence without pretending to be extroverts

- I'm Tim. I coach introverts on how to network without feeling awkward

- I'm Tim. I help enterprise clients work agile in a low-risk, high-value way in less than four weeks

- I'm Tim. I work in IT. I design websites and apps and make them easier to use

- I'm Tim. I work with early-stage start-ups with five or fewer designers to scale their hiring and operations

- I'm Tim. I'm a coach for designers. I help designers level up so managers can focus on business outcomes

Have more than one small introduction. When you have a few, you can choose the right one to use depending on your audience and situational context. For example:

- **If my local plumber asks what I do for a living**: I'd say "I work in IT…"

- **If I'm at an international design conference with product designers:** I'd say "I am a coach for designers…"

- **If I am at a tech networking event:** I'd say "I work with early-stage startups…"

Remember to practise your small introductions out loud. Words may look great on paper but sound unnatural when you say them. Prepare, practise, and iterate; use words and phrases that suit you.

Also, speak plainly. Use concrete terms, simple words, less jargon, and less business-speak. For example:

- **OK**: I create online experiences that delight customers and exponentially exceed a business's conversion rate outcomes.

- **Better**: I write words for webpages that tell customers exactly what they want to know so they buy more product.

Out of the three types of introductions, small introductions are the ones that I use most frequently. Invest your preparation and practise time on small introductions.

Medium introductions

A medium introduction is one to three minutes long. If in doubt, shorter is better.

Audiences and scenarios where a medium introduction is useful include:

- **You are the newest member of a group:** You are probably the only one introducing yourself, and most people are keen to learn who you are

- **You are the facilitator of a meeting or workshop:** You are introducing the agenda of the session

If it is your first day joining a new company and you are meeting your team for the first time, a medium introduction uses the following variables:

- Name

- Position (role, reporting line, peers)

- Prior experience, notable work

- Something personal

- Best way to reach you

For example:

> Hi, I'm Tim. I'm the new product designer in the Design Systems team working with my peers John and Jane and reporting up to Janice.

> Before joining this team, I worked at Company A and Company B. I helped scale their design systems globally from scratch in less than three months.

> Outside of work, I bind books, love coffee art, and have a 10 year-old Old English Sheepdog. If you are keen to get in touch, find me on Slack (@slack) or email (email@email.com).

Medium introductions are flexible. You can introduce, your role, or an activity. For example, if you were a facilitator of a workshop, you might say something like this:

> Hi, I'm Tim and I will be your facilitator for this workshop.

> For the next 60 minutes, our goal is to generate as many ideas as possible to solve the following problem: How might we encourage more users to download and sign in to our mobile app?

> For this session, all you will need are the pens and post-it notes in front of you. So if you can take a moment to put your laptops and notebooks away and turn your mobile phones to silent, that would be great.

> As your facilitator, I have one job and one job only: To get us to the outcome we want on time and on agenda. That means I may have to interrupt you, not because I'm not interested in what you have to say, but because I'm keen to keep us on track.

> Over here on the side, I have what I call a Parking Lot: If an interesting topic comes up during the session but it is off topic, I will write it on a post-it note and put it on the Parking Lot for you to continue the discussion later.

> Any questions before we start?

Large introductions

A large introduction is no longer than five minutes long. The audience is taken through the widest breadth of your role, your experience, who you are, how you work, and your notable accomplishments.

Audiences and scenarios where a large introduction is useful include:

- **Job interviews**: Broad sweep of your experience and notable accomplishments at the start of your interview

- **New manager of a team**: You are meeting your team for the first time

- **Joining a company on your first day**: Sharing a video recording of your introduction asynchronously

- **New boss**: You are meeting each other for the first time

Show and tell: Use visual aids to help tell your story. The more senses you use (e.g. sight, hearing), the clearer your message is communicated. To show and tell, you can:

- Project your slide deck onto a large screen

- Turn your laptop to face your audience

- Write or draw on a whiteboard or piece of paper

- Show a chronology of companies you've worked at and roles you've held

- Show notable pieces of work you have delivered and what they looked like before/after

Why no longer than five minutes? Because you do not know what the audience is interested in. You can guess, but unless you can read minds, you can never know for sure. The longer your introduction, the less time your audience has to dig deeper into areas that they are interested in.

Cannot do an introduction in less than five minutes? I promise: You can.

Firstly, do not speak faster to make up for time. Instead, show more, tell less: Use diagrams and images to help you tell your story. A picture is worth a thousand words.

Secondly, economise your words: How can you say the same thing with fewer words?

Lastly, edit ruthlessly. Ask yourself: If you met this person tomorrow, what are the one or two things you hope they remembered about you?

How can you decide between a medium or large introduction? Use a large introduction if you are the "main event": You are the primary reason why people have gathered, you are the primary message in the communication. If you are not the "main event," use a medium introduction instead.

The Menu

When people finish introducing themselves, they usually just stop talking. This would be OK if the audience was listening to every word you said. But audiences are easily distracted. If you just stop talking, audiences may struggle to think about what to talk about next.

As an alternative, finish your large introduction with The Menu. The Menu is a short list of two to three topics that you have curated as suggestions for the audience to talk about next. The Menu is only a suggestion; your audience may choose to talk about something completely different. For example, let's say you just ended a large introduction at an interview. You might say something like this:

> So that is a brief summary of my career. I have put together some examples of work I think you might be interested in. We can talk about:

> 1. How I set up a framework for running conversion rate experiments at a fast-growing start-up

> 2. How I hired and scaled up a team from one person to 10 people in six months

> 3. How I implemented a design system from scratch at an organisation that had incurred significant technical debt

> Or we can talk about something else. I will stop here and see what you would like to talk about next.

Like any good restaurant, never put anything on The Menu that you are not proud of. You curate The Menu. Your Menu is the best that you can offer to this audience. Prepare your Menu wisely.

Your audience can ask to explore other topics that are not on The Menu, but at least you came with a list of good options you prepared and practised for beforehand.

Let your audience ask curious follow-up questions

Think of your introduction like a movie trailer: Your goal is to pique the interest of the audience so they will go watch the movie.

You want to give the audience the broadest understanding of who you are—just the highlights. You do not want to share everything; it would take too long and you cannot be sure what the audience is really interested in.

Keep the audience wanting more and leave them plenty of time to dive deeper into topics that interest them. Give your audience space to ask curious follow-up questions.

Cannot think of anything to say about yourself? I had the same problem; I always found it more interesting to talk about other people than to talk about myself.

I then realised that I did not need to be interesting, I needed to be relatable. To be relatable, I needed to have things in common with my audience.

For ideas on how to be relatable, read the "Maslow's hierarchy of needs" section of the "Small Talk" chapter. Focus on the lower levels of the hierarchy; things at these levels have the broadest audience and highest chance of piquing interest in others. For example:

> I bind books by hand because I could never find the perfect notebook, so I learned to make my own.

> I live on a farm with our Old English Sheepdog and dream of building an introvert retreat here one day.

> I am the baker in our household and my specialities are Seeded Dark Rye Sourdough and Slivered Apple Tart.

I frequently sprinkle the words "bookbinding," "Old English Sheepdog," "farm," and "baking" in my introductions without going into detail, like loose threads in a woolly sweater that I leave for my audience to pull and ask curious follow-up questions about if they are interested.

Remember: Introducing yourself happens all the time, so it is worth practising and getting good at it. It is the one part of social interactions that you are most in control of.

This is your story. It is also people's first impression of you. Pique their interest. Leave them curious. Tell your story well.

Chapter 3

Small talk

> How are you?

> How was your weekend?

> Any plans for the holidays?

When it came to small talk, I seldom knew what to say or how much detail to share. Why would someone that I just met ask me how my weekend was? Should I really tell them that my car broke down and that I was caught in the rain, fell sick, and spent two days in bed? Should I really tell them that I plan to play PlayStation and watch Netflix over the holidays? How interested were they? Why would someone ask me how I was if they did not really want to know? Why would people say things they do not mean?

Like introductions, small talk usually happens at the start of a conversation. Unlike introductions, small talk is a conversation rather than a monologue. You are less in control because others are involved. I had to learn how to make small talk. Here is how.

Why do people make small talk?

Small talk is like a verbal handshake before the real conversation begins.

Imagine putting your hand out to shake and having the other person not notice or not shake your hand back. Awkward, isn't it? Same with small talk. When you do not make small talk, the other party feels like they have stuck their hand out for a handshake but you aren't shaking it back.

Small talk is not real talk; that comes after. Small talk is an opportunity to connect at a basic human level before the real conversation begins.

Pleasantries

Pleasantries usually happen at the very start of a conversation. Other times, small talk happens first. Be like water:[4] Go with the flow.

Every culture has their own version of pleasantries. I found the following the most common:

> Hello, my name is Tim.

> My name is John. Nice to meet you.

Or

Context is key. If the person greeting you is someone you just met or you do not have a deep relationship with, chances are they are not really asking how you are. They are simply saying hello.

With an acquaintance or colleague, pleasantries might continue on to small talk. For example:

How was your weekend?

Any plans for the holidays?

What do you do for a living?

Your response depends on context and how you feel in the moment:

If time is short or you do not feel like sharing:

How was your weekend?

Good; how was yours?

If you have time to spare and you feel like sharing to connect at a deeper level:

How was your weekend?

Great! We went fishing; the weather was beautiful and we each caught like 20 barramundi!

If you have no energy to actually explain what you do for a living:

What do you do?

I work in IT.

Brevity is key. You may attempt to be interesting, but let the person dig deeper if they are truly keen. The level of detail you choose to reveal depends on your relationship with the person and the conversation that is about to happen. You do not talk about a great weekend spent fishing before a performance review.

Practise saying your pleasantries out loud. Find the words that feel just right for you, words that you can say automatically, without thinking. These are likely words you already use.

Framework for small talk

Small talk, like most conversations, alternates between questions and statements. For example:

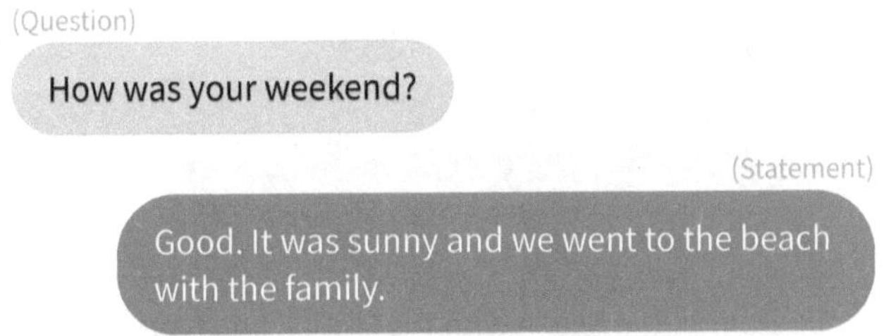

You do not always have to start with a question. You can also start with a statement and finish with a question. For example:

(Statement)

Gosh, it was so hot over the weekend.

(Question)

What did you get up to?

(Statement)

We went to the beach with the family, but everyone had the same idea and the beach was packed with people. We had fun though.

(Question)

How about you?

Alternate between questions and statements. If you keep asking question after question, it will feel like an interrogation rather than a conversation. For example:

(Question)

Gosh, it was so hot over the weekend. What did you get up to?

(Statement)

We went to the beach with the family, but everyone had the same idea and the beach was packed with people. We had fun though.

(Statement)

I wish that I had the same idea. We spent the weekend with the air conditioning on watching a movie marathon of oscar nominated movies.

(Question)

Interesting! What did you watch?

With small talk statements, alternate between facts and reveals.

Facts are irrefutable statements you believe to be true. For example:

> It was raining all weekend. We had almost 75 millimetres of rain over two days, more than the whole of last month!

Or

> I had to work over the weekend. John said the report was due on Monday morning.

Reveals are personal details or special pieces of information you choose to share. They tell others more about you or your situation, things you would not normally share with people you just met or do not know well. For example:

> It was 40 degrees celsius on Saturday. Luckily, we made plans to visit our friends who have a pool and it turned out to be a pretty great day out in the sun!

Or

> It was raining all weekend. It rained so much, our roof started to leak. One leak became two, then three. We actually ran out of buckets to handle the leaks and had to go buy more buckets.

Or

> I had to work over the weekend. John received a phone call from the CEO on Friday evening saying that the client had given him feedback on our draft report. The CEO promised to send an updated report to the client by Monday morning. It was not a fun weekend for me.

Reveals are essential for building connections

Reveals are pieces of information which you do not normally share with others.

If you are keen to build a connection with someone, keep going with questions and statements until the person shares a reveal. This can happen in one conversation or after multiple conversations over time.

Sometimes, you can share a reveal first. This requires good faith. This good faith shows the trust you have in the other person, which can encourage them to share a reveal after.

Trust can take time to earn. The other person may not choose to share a reveal in this conversation, but they might in the next one. If you are keen to build a connection with a person, trust first, keep going, and do not give up.

Build connections by remembering reveals

You build a deeper connection with someone when you mention their reveal the next time you have a conversation. This shows that you cared enough to remember. For example:

Conversation 1:

(Question)

Hey, how are you?

Good, yourself?

(Question)

Good, good. Man, it's freezing today, isn't it? Is it cold where you are?

It's not too bad. I'm just glad it isn't raining.

(Fact)

Yeah, like last week. It must have been about 75 millimetres of rain.

Gosh! That much? I didn't realise.

(Reveal)

Yeah. It rained so much, our roof started to leak.

Really? Did you manage to fix it?

(Reveal)

We tried, but I don't think it's going to last. Probably need a professional, but good ones are hard to find.

Tell me about it…

Conversation 2:

(Question)

Hey, how are you?

Good, yourself?

(Question)

Not too bad. Hey, how did your roof go? Did you manage to fix it?

I'm afraid not. In fact, it's gotten worse. It's started to mould.

(Fact)

Oh no! Plus, they're expecting heavy rain again.

Yes. I'm aware. Sucks to be me, right?

(Question)

I asked a few friends if they knew a good handyman and I got one contact. Would you like their number?

Wow, really? Sure!

Use Maslow's hierarchy of needs as a framework for small talk topics

Maslow's hierarchy of needs[5] is a theory of human motivation. It suggests that people are motivated to fulfil basic needs before they move up to other, more advanced needs further up the hierarchy.

It consists of five levels:

- **(Top)** Self-actualisation

- Esteem needs

- Love and belonging needs

- Safety needs

- **(Bottom)** Physiological needs

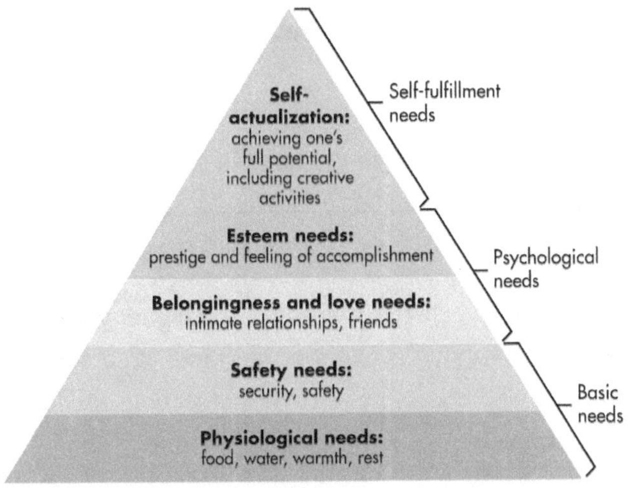

Diagram: Maslow's hierarchy of needs

You can use Maslow's hierarchy as a framework for coming up with small talk topics. At each level, develop a variety of small talk topics that suit you. For example:

- **Self-actualisation**: Ambitions, Dreams

- **Esteem needs**: Successes, Accomplishments

- **Love and belonging needs**: Pets, Sports, Family, Music, TV, Hobbies

- **Safety needs**: Health, Housing

- **Physiological needs**: Weather, Food, Sleep

Start at the bottom of Maslow's hierarchy and move up

Small talk topics based on the bottom of Maslow's hierarchy of needs have the widest applicability. We are all human, and those topics are our lowest common denominator.

The lower the level in the hierarchy, the higher your chances of having something in common and making a connection. Remember: You do not need to be interesting, you just need to be relatable.

You can make small talk with almost anyone about the weather or what they had for breakfast or lunch. Everyone needs to eat, drink, and sleep.

Your small talk topics can be positive, but they can also be negative. Life is not a bed of roses, and negative stories can make you relatable. For example:

- **Self-actualisation**: You were at your favourite rock band's concert last night and had an amazing time, but you wonder if that could have been your life too if you had picked a different path ("You know, I was in a rock band in high school...")

- **Esteem**: You were the champion of the arcade game *Space Invaders*, but over the weekend, your partner beat your high score (and they do not even like *Space Invaders*!)

- **Love and belonging**: Your favourite sports team, one

you have supported for years, lost the championship tournament over the weekend

- **Safety**: Your landlord raised the rent again and you might have to move because you can no longer afford to live there

- **Physiological**: You commuted to the office in the rain, so now you have wet socks and cold feet (nobody likes wet socks)

You only need two or three small talk topics

Do not overthink it. Keep it simple. Use the topics that come most naturally to you.

For example, I regularly complain about the weather. It is either too hot or too cold, too wet or too dry. Once in a while, the weather will be a perfect 24 degrees celsius with blue skies and partial sunshine, and I'll be full of praise. Even then, I can make small talk about how glorious the weather is.

I also bake and love food. Food travel documentaries are my guilty pleasure. My partner and I constantly struggle to decide what to cook for dinner, so I am always curious about what other people eat.

These topics come naturally to me, and I use the same topics over and over again in different conversations even with the same people—I just change the content. For example:

Love and belonging

1. **Pets** - "Our dog had to go to the vet's this morning. We think she has an ear infection; she keeps shaking her head all day long"

2. **Sports** - "Did you watch the game on Saturday? Wow, that was the best the team played all season!"

3. **Family** - "Our relatives flew in from overseas so I'm taking some time off this long weekend to show them around"

4. **Music** - "Have you heard Taylor Swift's new album? It sounds just like the last one!"

5. **TV** - "Did you watch that latest show on Netflix? Be careful: once you start, you can't stop!"

Safety

1. **Chores** - "We had to clear out the garden this weekend. We have had so much rain, the weeds grew like crazy and just took over!"

2. **Shelter** - "I'm so glad we added a fireplace to our living room. It was so cold over the weekend; the fireplace really warmed up the house"

Physiological

1. **Weather** - "Is it sunny where you are? 'Cos it rained all weekend over here"

2. **Food** - "We had Mexican last night; I could eat Mexican food for every meal"

3. **Sleep** - "I'm so glad the baby slept through the night. I feel like a new man!"

Use your senses to mine for small talk topics on the spot

If no small talk topic comes to mind immediately, you can always use your senses (sight, sound, touch, smell, taste) to notice and respond to something that is happening to you or your audience in the moment. This can be done in real life or virtually. Always be aware of your surroundings.

For example, in a virtual meeting:

- **Sight**: "I'm looking out your window in the background and I can see it's snowing!"; "Gosh, is it summer over there in Australia? We are in the depths of winter in the USA right now—wish I was there!"

- **Hearing**: "Is there someone at your door? I can hear your dog barking"; "I can still hear drilling noises in your background. When is your neighbour completing their renovation work?"

Learning how to introduce yourself and make small talk has the most impact in the long run

I was once asked during a podcast interview: "Out of all the tiny habits, which have had the most impact?"

My reply surprised the host: I said one was the humble ability to introduce myself with confidence, and the other was avoiding social awkwardness by being able to comfortably make small talk with just about anyone. These interactions happen the most frequently, and over time, that impact adds up.

These two tiny habits opened doors and possibilities. They broadened the range of people who I could connect with. I avoided countless awkward silences, so others felt comfortable working with me. Getting good at these two habits allowed me to confidently connect with new people and deepen existing relationships. I could connect with people at a simple human level. The more people I met, the wider my network grew, and the deeper the relationships I formed became.

Since 2021, I've coached quiet achievers and run online courses on topics like public speaking, how to say no (politely), how to be more visible in your organisation, networking, facilitating workshops, handling difficult conversations, leading and managing teams, performing well in interviews, and many more.

These are areas that quiet achievers struggle with the most. They are high-stakes, important events and have high impact—but they also occur less frequently over the length of your career. We do not have difficult conversations every day. We do not facilitate workshops every day. We do not engage in public speaking every day.

However, on most days, we do have meetings. We have to work with colleagues to get the job done. We bump into our bosses at the pantry, at the water-cooler, or along the office corridor. These interactions always begin with introductions and small talk, and they happen almost every day. Frequency wins.

I suspect people neglect practising their introductions and developing small talk topics because it seems so trivial. They would rather focus on the hard stuff. I am here to tell you: The hard stuff is important, but do not underestimate the power of small talk and how to introduce yourself well. In the long run, these two tiny habits will help you have the most impact. It's a numbers game. Tiny habits, done well, accumulated over time.

Chapter 4

Meetings

You are in a meeting. The conversation meanders; you listen intently and try to follow along and process your thoughts at the same time. Suddenly, with no warning, someone says, "What do you think, [your name]?"

Your heart skips a beat. You look up, emerging from your deep cloud of thought. You were paying attention and following the conversation just fine. But as soon as your name was called, your mind went blank. That clever idea that was forming goes *poof!* and disappears.

All eyes around the room are on you now. You feel the burn of their gaze; you feel like a deer (or kangaroo) in headlights. Blood drains from your face. Your chest tightens; you feel faint. You clear your throat, and a nervous cough leaves your body.

You have no idea what to say.

You make some weird noises. All you manage is "Erm...I don't know...I'm not sure. What was the question again?"

Then, someone else jumps in and speaks (THANK YOU!). Your mind is still racing, your heart is still pounding. You do not fully register what that other person is saying, but it sure sounds like THAT thought you *just* had in your head.

And just like that, the moment passes.

You feel safe now that the eyes in the room are no longer upon you. You feel relief, but you also feel regret: *What's wrong with me? Why didn't I say something? Why didn't I speak up? Why does this happen every time? Sure, my response was not fully formed, it probably was not even that clever. But it is definitely better than saying "I don't know."*

You feel embarrassed. You feel like you lost face, lost a little respect from your peers. You feel like you missed an opportunity.

You wish you'd spoken up. You wish you'd said something. You wish you could do it over again.

Sound familiar?

Being put on the spot is always hard. Your emotions rise, your thoughts get clouded. The truth is, that feeling never goes away completely. The main thing that will change is knowing that feeling will come and feeling ready for it with tiny habits to use in meetings.

Why speak up in meetings?

In the Asian society I grew up in, you only speak up if you have something meaningful to say or something to add to the conversation. To say something wrong, silly, half-baked, or not fully thought through can result in you "losing face" and reducing your reputation.

In other cultures, participation equals interest. If you do not participate, you are not interested. It matters less if what you say is wrong, silly, or smart. It matters more that you participate and contribute.

The common thread in such cultures is this: When you speak up, you are invested. The outcome now affects you because you have skin in the game.

If you do not speak up—if you think the group's direction is wrong but say nothing—you have the quiet satisfaction of thinking *I knew it* when things do not go to plan. But now, your team has failed.

This is not the behaviour of a team player. When you speak up and participate, especially when you participate well, you become a team player.

Another reason to speak up: You were invited to the meeting for a reason. People in the room are keen to have you involved. If they did not want you involved, they would not have invited you in the first place.

One final reason to speak up in meetings: People cannot read minds (yet)! If you do not speak up, if you do not share your thoughts, no one will ever know what you are thinking.

Buy yourself time

I usually need time to think before I speak, while others speak in order to think.

If you are like me and need time to think before you speak: There is nothing wrong with you. You just need a little more time to process your thoughts before you share them. The overarching strategy is to buy yourself time. Here are a few tiny habits to do that.

Repeat the other person's question out loud

Repeating back a question someone has asked you out loud, in your own voice, can help you formulate a response. It will feel like you are asking yourself the question, so you hear the question again as if it was inside your head. For example:

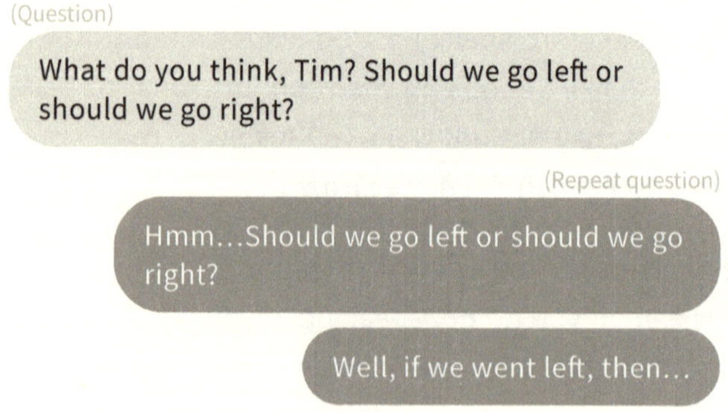

Ask the other person to repeat or rephrase the question

Sometimes, when people think out loud, their thoughts meander down a long winding path before they arrive at a question (if at all). In this situation, the question may not be clear to either of you.

Asking the other person to repeat or rephrase the question gives them—and you—an opportunity to sharpen and clarify the question. For example:

> I do not understand the question; do you mind rephrasing?

> Wow…that train of thought went to so many places. Do you mind asking your question again, please?

> Do you mind asking the question again, but rephrasing or using simpler words?

> I was thinking deeply about what you said earlier. Do you mind asking your question again, please?

Give yourself permission and a licence to speak up

Sometimes you are in a meeting and someone asks a question. It is an interesting question, one that catches your attention.

Your brain is on it; the gears are turning. Ideas are emerging, and you can see the shape of your answer, but it is cloudy, not fully formed.

All of a sudden, someone in the room calls your name and says, "[Your name], what do you think?"

Blood drains from your face. Your mind is racing. You are not ready. That great idea that was still forming in your head? It is gone! You make some excuse, some nervous noises, and then the attention passes on to someone else. And you are kicking yourself for not speaking up.

How do you speak up before you are ready?

You need to give yourself permission to speak up, a licence to speak even though you aren't ready. It could sound something like this:

> This might sound really silly, but I'm going to say it anyways…

> You probably know this already, but…

> What I am about to say is not fully formed yet, but here is what I have so far…

> I do not know if I fully believe what I'm about to say, but this is what I have in my mind right now…

Prefacing what you are about to say gives you permission and a licence to say it, even if you are not 100 percent ready or your thoughts are not fully formed yet. It lowers the stakes in case what you say turns out to be wrong or silly.

The important thing is getting your thought or idea out there so someone else can build upon it. You have participated, you have skin in the game; you are now a team player.

Defer

When the "microphone" is passed to us in a meeting, we assume that we must speak up then and there, even if we are not ready.

That is like a waiter in a restaurant asking if you are ready to order, but you are not. It is perfectly acceptable to ask for a few more minutes. You can defer.

In a meeting, you can say something like:

You're basically trying to say: "Not now, almost there. Come back later, please."

Actively listen and take notes

In meetings, focusing is essential, but hard: Not only are you listening to what others are saying, you are also processing your own thoughts at the same time.

Taking notes provides a visual record of your own thoughts and the discussion in the meeting so far. If your mind goes blank, you have something to look at to support your train of thought and get back on track.

These notes are not meeting minutes. Their purpose is to facilitate your own thinking. Use notations, draw ideas, make to-do lists, write deadlines, assign next steps. You are the only one looking at these notes. Take notes in ways that best serve you.

Train yourself to signal when you have something to say

Sometimes, you have something to say, but something holds you back. Perhaps you have never enjoyed the spotlight, when everyone's eyes are on you. It's easier to keep quiet and swallow your words. But what you have to say is important and meaningful.

In moments like these, train yourself to signal that you have something to say. You could raise your hand or send a chat message in your virtual meeting room (e.g. "I have something that I'd like to share. Can I speak next?").

Doing this shifts your thinking from making excuses *not* to speak up to focusing on *how* you are going to say what you want to say. Signal early; the longer you wait, the less likely it is that you will speak up.

Remember: You were invited to the meeting for a reason. To participate in the discussion is to be a team player. So speak up to become a player on the team.

Review the agenda and prepare talking points beforehand

Every meeting should have an agenda. Not having an agenda is like going grocery shopping without a list when you are hungry: You end up with many things you do not need but none of the things you do.

No meeting agenda? Ask the meeting organiser beforehand what the purpose of the meeting is and what is going to be discussed. Then, write down things you would like to talk about or questions you want to ask. Have this ready before the meeting starts.

Arrive to meetings early

The one thing that remains true about both virtual meetings and meetings in real life is that there is always someone who is late: Someone you are waiting for so that the meeting can finally begin. There is no point in starting the meeting because you are just going to have to repeat what you said all over again when the late person finally arrives.

So why arrive early? You should arrive early because in this small pocket of time, you are alone with the punctual attendees. Everyone will arrive at a different time, so being early often gives you precious 1:1 time to connect with the people you work with. Sometimes it is your teammates who are early. Other times it's your boss, or your boss's boss.

You can use this time to practise small talk. For example:

What did you have for lunch?

Is that a new shirt?

How did your partner's interview go?

The minutes between meetings are when people speak more freely, because there is nobody else there to listen. It's an opportunity to connect on a more personal level.

By arriving early, you get to ask people how they truly are. You might never have that opportunity if you arrive late.

The best meeting is a 1:1

Make most of your meetings 1:1. In 1:1s, you only have to focus on one person instead of a group of people competing for attention.

More importantly, they are away from the public eye. People are more open to being wrong when no one is looking. They are also more open to telling you what they really think when nobody else is listening.

You might be thinking: *Wait, would it not be more efficient if we just had everyone at one big meeting to talk about this one thing?*

Or: *Wait, 1:1s with everyone? That's a LOT of meetings, and so much more work!*

The answer to both of these questions is yes. However, group meetings are rife with difficult-to-navigate social dynamics. Plus, the more people in a meeting, the harder it is to find a time slot that suits everyone. Finally, it is easier to steer one person than a crowd of people, especially if group meetings are not your thing.

When planning your calendar, include time to recharge between meetings

Unlike extroverts, quiet achievers often lose energy with social interactions. We need time between social sessions to recharge.

Plus, truly good work requires focus time for deep work. If your job requires deep work, then going from one meeting to another, day after day, is not the best way to get things done. You will spend all your time context switching rather than focusing on the task at hand.

Try this instead: Divide your calendar into meeting-heavy days (e.g. Mon, Wed, Fri) and meeting-light days (e.g. Tues, Thurs). Treat your meeting-light days with respect. Draw boundaries. Block out time in your calendar for deep work. Guard that deep work time with your life. Do not accept meetings on meeting-light days unless they are truly important and urgent.

You may not be in a position to manage your own calendar. This is usually true when you are starting out in your career and your role is lower down in the organisational hierarchy. In this case, be sure that your boss is aware of your practices, knows why you do them, and accepts them. When you find yourself in a position to exert influence on a project or team's calendar of activities, use that influence to make the calendar suit you.

High-stakes meetings

A high-stakes meeting is one where an ultimate decision has to be made. It is a go or no-go decision. Chances are, your boss is there and your boss's boss is too, and the people in the room have strong opinions and loud voices.

So, as a quiet achiever, what do you do?

I have been to a few of these high-stakes meetings, and I think there is a secret to them. The secret is this: People who attend these meetings have most likely made up their minds before the meeting even starts.

So the tactic here is to influence the outcome before the meeting, not during it.

Let us think about the audience for a moment:

1. High-stakes meetings usually involve senior executives

2. Senior executives usually have more experience

3. Senior executives also tend to have more things to focus on and less time to make decisions

4. Very rarely will a single decision truly break a company. It's usually a series of poor decisions that will break a company

Therefore, senior executives will lean on their prior experience to help them make decisions quickly.

In my experience, once these decisions are solidified in their minds, it is very hard to change them. So to influence the outcome of a high-stakes meeting, have 1:1 meetings hours, days, weeks, or even months before the meeting: The higher the stakes, the further in advance.

The goal is to influence their thinking before they make up their minds. You get to explain your position and your rationale. You can also ask what they think—and, as I mentioned earlier, if it is a 1:1, people will be more open to being wrong or saying "I don't know."

For example, at these 1:1 meetings, you could talk about:

- **Feedback on early ideas**: "It is still early days and we have not finished our research yet. But two ideas have emerged that I have a good feeling about. Can I tap into your expertise and get your first impressions?"

- **Reacting to news**: "What you said the other day at the company all-hands meeting really struck a chord with me. As you were speaking, an idea for our product came to mind and I started sketching it out. Can I show it to you and see what you think?"

Think of it like steering a container ship. A container ship takes 20 minutes to come to a complete stop. So if you want to change the course of a container ship, you have to start steering early. Really early.

Not everything has to be a meeting

Meetings are not always the best way to get things done.

For one thing, meetings are synchronous (live, real time), which means attendees need to be present at a fixed date, time, and place—and the more attendees you invite, the harder it is to find a time when everyone is available.

If you work with a globally-distributed team and need to meet virtually across time zones, it will always be too early or too late for someone who is attending (if they even show up).

Also, meetings are rife with politics, posturing, and power struggles. Some teams even encourage adversarial behaviour, claiming that conflict leads to better decisions. Remember: The louder voices may seem to say the most, but do not always have the most to say.

Meeting this way is not just bad for quiet achievers, it is bad for most of us.

If you are planning a meeting where one or two people are delivering monologues with little to no interaction with the rest of the attendees, there might be a better way to get things done.

Consider asynchronous (not live, at a time you decide) methods to get things done. That could be an email, a text message, or a well-written post on an instant messaging platform like Slack.

However, writing well takes time. It also takes skill to replicate the same level of emotion, tone, and conviction that happens in verbal communication with only the written word.

So if not meetings and not writing, then what?

Record a short video of yourself

Instead of a monologue during a meeting where you present your point of view, why not record a video of yourself doing the same thing so that your audience can watch it in their own time?

I will admit, you will cringe the first few times you rewatch a video of yourself. It may even take a few tries before you get a good take. The problem is most people do not persevere; they give up before they get good, before they cross the tipping point.

I call this tipping point The Hump (named after the humpback of a camel).

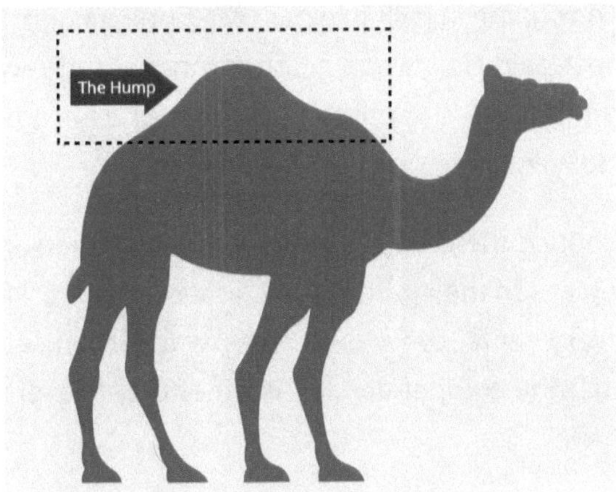

Diagram: Hump of a camel

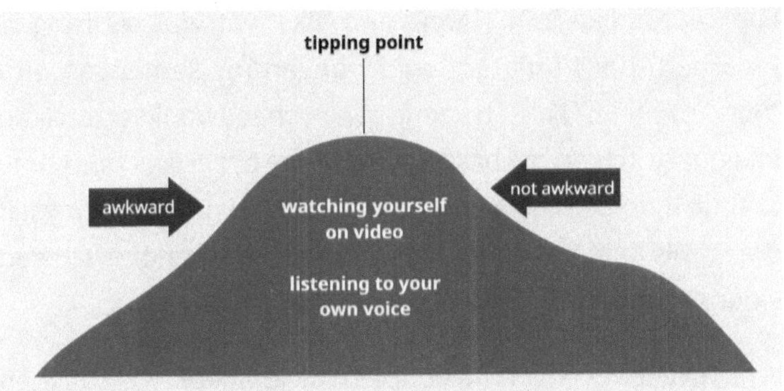

Diagram: The tipping point where watching or listening to yourself is no longer awkward

I guarantee this: The initial discomfort of watching yourself on video will pass. The key is to keep going till you cross that tipping point; do not give up. You will know you have crossed the tipping point when you stop noticing that it is you in the video. Thereafter, rewatching a video of yourself will feel like watching any other talking head on TV or YouTube.

There is no shame in failing to pass the tipping point: Some of the highest-paid Hollywood actors cannot stand rewatching their own movies. The problem is most of us are not highly-paid Hollywood actors.

You will notice the greatest managers and players in sports watch replays of their game. They dissect every tackle, every swing, every serve, every pass. They watch themselves and they watch the competition, all in an effort to level up their own game.

Rewatching a video of yourself is a great way to get better at public speaking. You notice the little tics and habits you have when you speak. For example, I noticed that I used filler words like "um," "aah," and "like" without realising it. I learned that I unintentionally began my sentences with "now" or "next." I also became aware that I would scratch an imaginary itch on my belly and raise my eyebrows from time to time (I do not know why I did that). I did not notice myself doing this in the moment. I only noticed it when I rewatched videos of myself.

What ever bad habits you notice in these videos, you can then fix, iterate, and improve upon them for your next recording. You are not changing who you are; you simply want to show up as the best version of yourself.

Plus, no one sees your bad videos; they only see your best video. You will have all the time in the world to practise, reflect, and deliver a thoughtful, polished presentation in a safe environment.

Once you've recorded a video, you can share it multiple times for others to watch at their convenience. This saves you time from presenting the same thing to different people over multiple meetings.

When others share your videos, you become more visible in your organisation. People you do not know personally will know about you and your work.

Some possible scenarios of use:

- **Asking for feedback on something you made**: Let us say you made a new iteration of a design or a report. You can record a short video of yourself presenting what is new and specifying where you would like (and not like) feedback. Set a reasonable deadline for responses. Your audience can reply in their own time once they have had time to collect their thoughts. They could even record a short video of themselves with feedback on your work

- **Daily/Fortnightly/Monthly updates**: Daily update meetings, or standup meetings,[6] are part of the way agile technology teams work. Individuals recount what they did yesterday, what they are going to do today, and whether they faced any issues. Leaders and managers may be asked to provide updates on their teams and products/projects at company-wide events. All of the above are monologues, and can be replaced with short videos

- **Recognition and appreciation**: People like being appreciated in different ways. Some like the biggest stage with the largest audience and maximum visibility of colleagues and peers witnessing when they are told "You are awesome!" Others, like me, prefer a personal, heartfelt "Well done!" given directly and in private. If the recipient appreciates it, you could even do both! But a short video recording can be played back, and reminds the recipient they are appreciated when they need to hear it the most

When making these videos:

- **Keep it short (five minutes or less)**: Your audience has limited time and a short attention span. Get straight to the point and share only the highlights. Think TikTok, not *Lord of the Rings*. If in doubt, shorter is better

- **Add links**: When sharing the video, add links and attachments to details. Not everything has to be in the video

- **Show and tell**: Share your screen, show the work. Use visual aids to help tell your story

- **Show your face**: This is important. You need to be associated with the work being shown on the screen. The easiest way to do this is to place a picture-in-picture video of yourself talking about the work in the corner of the video when recording. This way, you become the face of that work

- **Keep going till you get a good take**: There are two ways to get a good take. The first option is to edit a collection of your videos and stitch the good bits together to form one good take. The second is to keep recording till you get a good take. The former requires more post-production effort and makes you a better video editor. The latter requires more public speaking practise and makes you a better public speaker. Choose the latter

- **Stream the video via a link**: Make it easy for others to watch your video immediately. Some platforms automatically upload your video and provide a link ready for you to share with others. Other platforms require you to record your video, export a large file, upload your video, make a cup of tea while you wait for the upload to complete, then share your video. Choose the platform that offers the quickest route to sharing the video

Recording short videos of yourself allows you to perform when you are at your best.

Chapter 5

Public speaking

Early in my career, I was responsible for designing a website. I noticed users were struggling to buy product online, so I led the work to design a more effective solution. It tested well and it was a design our engineers liked because it was elegant and low effort to build.

We went live with the new design in record time and the results were successful beyond any of our expectations. Customers were buying product at a significantly higher rate. It was a great example of going from insight to execution in a short amount of time. Customers were happy. The company was happy. Our team was happy. Win-win-win.

This caught the attention of our senior leadership team, and they wanted us to present our work at the company all-hands meeting the following week. Everyone in the company would be there. Everyone.

They asked us who would like to present the work. I felt as if the whole team was looking at me, but no one said the words.

The voice in my head kept saying: *I should present it. I led the work and I know it inside out. I should do it.*

But the thought of standing in front of our whole company made my heart skip a beat. I could already see the faces of everyone in the company looking at me, waiting for me to speak. I froze.

The voice in my head continued: *It is not enough time for me to prepare. I still have all this other work do, there is no way I can take on this presentation. What if I forget what I was going to say? Everyone will stare at me. What if I make a fool of myself? I would be letting the whole team down.*

I felt lightheaded. It felt like minutes passed in silence, but in reality it was seconds. I knew that I should be the one to present the work, but I could not bring myself to say "yes."

"I am happy to present if no one else would like to do it?" said Jane, the product manager, after a long, awkward silence.

Instantly, I felt relief. I felt like the pressure was off me. Jane was a good presenter and would do a great job.

But I also felt regret. I had been responsible for this work. I should have spoken up for it. I truly appreciated Jane stepping up to present the work, but I was disappointed in myself for letting another public speaking opportunity pass me by.

This had happened before. This had happened many times over my career, and I was tired of feeling this way. I was ready to change.

Why is public speaking important?

We live in a world where the extrovert ideal is desired. Even with technology and social media, public speaking remains one of the best ways for us to broadcast our thoughts and ideas. We speak up on behalf of our work, and there is no one who can do it better than us.

The first thing you need to know about public speaking is that it is a skill. Skills can be practised. With practise, you get better and it gets easier. You just have to start.

The second thing you should know about public speaking is that speaking well is not a reflection of your substance, nor does it represent the quality of the thing that you are speaking about. You do not have to be smart to speak well. You might sound smarter, but it does not mean that you *are* smarter.

Want proof? Listen to Soundgarden's "Black Hole Sun":[7] A melody that makes you sit up and listen. Guitar riffs that make the hair on the back of your neck stand up. The late Chris Cornell's voice of an angel. Here is a sample of the lyrics:

In my eyes
Indisposed
In disguises no one knows
Hides the face
Lies the snake
And the sun in my disgrace

Boiling heat
Summer stench
'Neath the black, the sky looks dead
Call my name
Through the cream
And I'll hear you scream again

Black hole sun
Won't you come
And wash away the rain?
Black hole sun
Won't you come
Won't you come
Won't you come

Great song, amazing musician. But Chris did not intend for the words to mean anything. He was playing with words for words' sake. There was no real idea to get across.

Three types of scripts

There are three type of scripts you can prepare for public speaking events:

1. **Introduction script**: Just the first two to three minutes of your public speaking event

2. **Bullet points**: Key points you want to make, things you want the audience to remember and take away by the end of the session

3. **Full script**: Word-for-word everything that you will say and how you will say it

The type of script you use will depend on how much time you have to prepare and how high the stakes are. For example:

- **Introduction script**: Use at the ad-hoc workshop you have been asked to facilitate on short notice

- **Bullet points**: Use at the weekly team meeting, when you want to remind team members about the key objectives of the project

- **Full script**: Use at the high-stakes, company-wide event that is filmed in front of hundreds of people and where you have a time limit of exactly seven minutes

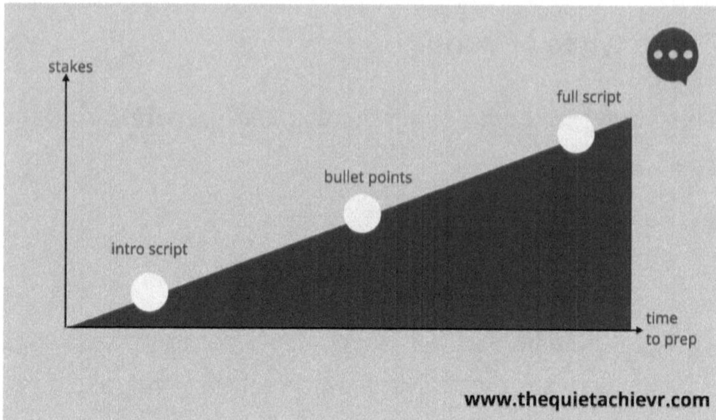

Diagram: The type of script you choose depends on how high the stakes are and how much time you have to prepare

Do not over-prepare or under-prepare. Choose the right level of scripting for the event. If you prepare a full script for an ad-hoc workshop you are facilitating, the conversation might meander in unpredictable directions, rendering your script less useful. If you prepare an introduction script for a high-stakes event where you only have seven minutes to speak, you might not remember all the content you want to cover in the time that you have, or you might go overtime.

Introduction script

An introduction script contains what you want to say to start off in the first two to three minutes of an event.

Some possible scenarios of use:

- Facilitating a workshop

- Running a retrospective

- Presenting a design for review

Information usually includes:

- Name

- Designation or role

- Agenda/purpose of session

- How long the activity will take

- "Any questions before we start?"

For example:

Hi, I'm Tim. Thank you all for coming to this ideation workshop for Project X. For the next 30 minutes, our goal is to generate as many ideas as possible to solve Problem Y.

We will not be evaluating the ideas you come up with in this session; we will evaluate them after. My role as facilitator is to get us to the end of this session on time and on agenda.

That means I may have to interrupt you occasionally, not because I am not interested in what you have to say, but so we can stay on track. All you will need for the next 30 minutes are the sharpies and post-it notes in front of you, so you can put away your laptops and mobile phones.

Any questions before we get started?

Bullet points

Bullet points are just the key points you want to make during the event. Think of them as the things you want the audience to take away by the time you are done talking.

Bullet points give you flexibility. You can choose the words you want to say as you are saying them, so your performance sounds more natural. This script is not a monologue. It works best for events where you may be interrupted and there is very little you can do about it.

Some possible scenarios of use:

- You are a participant in a brainstorming workshop and you have prepared some ideas to share beforehand so you are ready when it is your turn to speak

- You are presenting key insights from your work; your audience is seeing this for the first time and may have questions as you are presenting

When preparing your bullet point script:

- Brevity is key

- Make your bullet points easy to scan by starting each bullet point with keywords like "deadline," "objective," "constraints," etc. Alternatively, start bullet points with the first few words you want to say when you start speaking

- Write down key phrases you want to say and specific words you want to use

- Do not use full sentences—they are hard to scan in the brief moments you glance at your bullet points while you are speaking. Also, the actual words you choose to use in the moment may change. Writing full sentences locks you into only one way of saying things. Writing down only keywords gives you flexibility

- It is OK if no one else understands your bullet points. The only person looking at your bullet points is you; the only person they need to make sense to is you

Next, practise. Pretend you are speaking at the event. You do not have to close your eyes; just imagine the audience is in front of you. Start speaking, and glance at your bullet points when you need to. As you are practising, better words and new bullet points may come to mind. Edit and iterate.

Resist the temptation to polish bullet points to the point that they become a full script with full sentences. If you are doing this right now: Just stop. Remember: This script is not a monologue. You may be interrupted. Important points only. Flexibility is key.

Full script

A full script is, word-for-word, everything that you will say and how you will say it. It is a monologue that lasts longer than five minutes. Emphasis on *monologue*. You will not be taking questions, you are not allowing interruptions. You are delivering your full script from start to finish.

Every minute of a full script takes me an hour to prepare, so a 20-minute talk would take 20 hours to prepare (your mileage may vary). Few events require this level of preparation. Use full scripts sparingly, for only the highest of stakes. They are a huge investment.

Some possible scenarios of use:

- A talk in front of a large audience that you are likely to deliver more than once

- High-stakes presentation to your boss's boss's boss

To prepare a full script:

- Start with bullet points, then expand

- If a visual aid like a PowerPoint presentation is allowed, use it

- Write how you speak

- Speak out loud, not just in your head

- Focus on getting a rough first draft done from start to finish—you can polish later

Next, practise. Read the script from start to finish. You know you are sufficiently practised when the words come out of your mouth automatically: As you finish one sentence, the next one comes to mind. It is OK to still glance at your script, but you know you are ready when you glance only a handful of times.

As an example, this is what happened when I was preparing and practising my full script for a 20-minute talk at a conference:

- I wrote my script and prepared my slide deck

- I practised at my desk with my slide deck and script

- My drive to work was 30 minutes each way. I would practise my script from start to finish while I drove to work and back. No screens, no script—purely from memory, twice a day

- Sometimes, I'd forget a section. In the moment, I'd move on and just keep going till the end of the script. Then I'd practise the section I forgot when I was next at my desk

- As I practised, I sometimes found better ways of saying things which felt more natural; I revised my script accordingly

- It took me two weeks of this daily practise to confidently recite my script

Why do you need to practise so much? During the event, your primary focus will be on connecting and communicating with your audience. This is true for both in-person and remote events. Your full attention will be on your performance and making sure your message is connecting with the audience. It is harder (but not impossible) to connect with your audience if you are looking down and reading from a full script.

Something unexpected might happen as you are performing, and you will need to adapt. Or a new idea might come to you while you are presenting, so you want to improvise and add the idea to your script. Maybe the audience doesn't understand what you are trying to say, and you need to say something differently or come up with a different example on the spot.

Your attention will be fully consumed by all of this, and you will need to stay present in the moment; the last thing you need is to struggle to remember what you have to say next.

As good as scripts are, they are ultimately just supports. They help you get better at public speaking, but they do not automatically make you a better public speaker. To improve your performance as a public speaker, try the following tiny habits.

Speak slower

If you do nothing else and want to get better at public speak-ing, simply speak slower.

When we are nervous or excited, there is an energy within us that feels like it is bursting to get out. Words are coming out of our mouths at a speed that our brains cannot catch up with. When we are scared, anxious, surprised, or in an emotionally-heightened state, our emotions take over and our brains cannot process the right words to say.

As a result, we find ourselves saying things we do not mean, choosing words that were not quite right, or—worse—saying the wrong things unintentionally.

Afterwards, we think: *Why did I say that? That was so stupid. What was I thinking?*

We were not thinking; we were reacting to our emotions and we were speaking too fast for our brains to catch up.

The easiest way to get better at public speaking is to simply speak slower. Do not change what you have to say, do not change the tone you use to say it. Just slow down and take your time to enunciate and pronounce every single word as if it is the last word you will ever say.

Speaking slower lets your brain catch up to the speed at which words are leaving your mouth. It also helps audiences keep up with you and understand you better. You get to think more intentionally about the words you are choosing to say.

You also get to breathe. It is as if the world has gone into slow motion: Your thoughts are no longer racing to get out of your head, and your emotional peaks become manageable.

Vary your speaking speed to create emphasis

When you speak slowly, it creates a sharp contrast to when you speak quickly. That difference in speed can be used effectively to capture the audience's attention. The enemy of good, captivating public speaking is: a monotonous, evenly-paced cadence of speech.

Slow down to really emphasise the most important points you want to make. In between you can speed up all you want, because it is really just filler words before you slow down and make your next important point.

Put words you want to SAY with emphasis in ALL CAPS in your script

In your script, there will be words or phrases you want to say with emphasis. Write these words in ALL CAPS. This reminds you to emphasise those words WHEN you are saying them in the moment, rather than just relying on your memory.

Use pauses and silence

Speaking nonstop is tiring for both the speaker and the audience. One reason why people talk nonstop is because they are afraid of awkward silences. They would rather fill the silence with words, or just end abruptly, than endure an awkward silence. I believe awkward silences come from within: We either sense awkwardness in others, or we project our own feelings of awkwardness onto our audience.

In reality, I find that silence simulates connection—even when that connection is not really there. Think about the people you are most connected with or closest to. In their company, you are not speaking all of the time. You can sit there in total silence, doing your own thing, and it does not feel awkward at all. Getting comfortable with silence is contextual and learned.

By using silence, you simulate the natural flow of conversation that you'd have with people you are most comfortable with. You simulate connection, even if the connection is not really there.

A great way to use silence is to pause. You can pause after making an important point, in order to let that point really sink in. You can pause to take a sip of water; you can pause to take a deep breath.

When practising your script out loud, good moments to pause will present themselves. At these moments, write ---PAUSE--- in your script. During your live performance, this will signal where you want to pause intentionally so you do not have to worry about remembering when to pause.

Repeat key points for emphasis

Repeat key points for emphasis.
REPEAT key points for EMPHASIS.

Saying a phrase or sentence at least twice creates emphasis. For example:

> You need to take one pill, twice a day. I repeat: ONE pill, TWICE a day.

You can also ask yourself a question out loud, then answer it. The audience will feel like you are asking them the question and they need to answer it, increasing the chances of them remembering it. For example:

> You need to take one pill, twice a day. How many times do you need to take the pills? ---PAUSE--- ONE pill, TWICE a day.

Say: "I can think of three things. Number one..."

When a question is asked and you are about to reply, start by stating the number of points you want to make.

For example, you could say:

Sometimes, you do not have three points to make. Sometimes, you have three points but you forget the third one as you are speaking. That is OK. In this scenario, you can say, "Number three—there is no Number three" or "It just slipped my mind—I will share it later if I can remember what it is."

Other times, you can just start without calling out the number of things you want to say, like: "I can think of the following: Number one…Number two…"

Numbering the points you want to make has the following benefits:

1. It makes you sound knowledgeable, wise and considered

2. It makes you sound like you have thought things though (which you probably have anyways)

3. It gives your audience an indication of when you will be done speaking and when they can join the conversation next. If you said you are going to make three points, they will get ready to speak up as you are finishing point number three.

Indicate how long you intend to speak

Before speaking up, indicate how long you intend to speak.

This is especially helpful with meetings over video conference where only one person can speak at a time. And it can sound something like this:

> Can I take 30 seconds to share something important before we all break for lunch?

> If I can have two more minutes to cover this one last slide and make my final point?

Doing this has the following benefits:

- If the time you call out is short, others are less likely to interrupt you and more likely to give you the time you have asked for

- It indicates to others in the room, time-wise, when they might be able to speak up next

- Even if you go over the time you asked for, no one will really know because on most occasions no one is keeping track of time

Say "yes" to a public speaking opportunity that you know will be good for you

Sometimes, the opportunity to speak publicly presents itself. Often, it is an opportunity to present your work or the work of your team. You know you are the right person to do this, you know this opportunity is good for you, but you are nervous; something holds you back.

Your brain starts coming up with excuses not to do it: *It is too soon, I do not have enough time to prepare!*; *I have too much to do, my other deadlines are too tight for me to take this extra work on!*; *Oh no, I feel sick; I must be falling ill!*

When you know the opportunity is good for you, train yourself to say, like a reflex:

> Yes! I will do it!

Instantly, your mind's focus shifts from making up excuses not to do it to: *OK, I have just said yes. What do I need to do to be ready?*

Putting yourself out there takes courage. Growth begins with a single step. The nerves you were feeling will still be there. However, with the tiny habits you have practised in this chapter, you will be 10 times more ready than you were before.

Start with low stakes. Your skills will improve with practise and with every speaking opportunity you take; your skills will *not* improve if you do not take opportunities.

Each of the tiny habits in this chapter will only help you improve at public speaking incrementally. But when you choose the right script, speak slower, use pauses and silences, vary the speed with which you speak to create emphasis, indicate how long you intend to speak, and say yes to speaking opportunities, your performance will improve exponentially. Remember: Tiny habits, done well, accumulated over time.

Chapter 6

Handling difficult conversations

And just like that, the CEO walked out of the meeting room.

The team and I were stunned. We had spent two months preparing for the marketing campaign, and the deadline was in five days.

We had done everything right. We tested the designs with customers and refined our marketing campaign. Every two weeks, we showed the CEO early versions of our work to get his feedback and keep him informed. We did not want any surprises. But now, we were facing a roadblock, with no clear path forward.

The team was deflated. We did not know what to do next. How were we going to meet the deadline? What does "make it pop" even mean?

A difficult conversation needed to be had. As the leader of the team, I needed to handle it.

I met with the CEO later that day. We spoke about the designs, and I finally understood what "make it pop" meant. I knew how to fix it. However, I left the *real* difficult conversation unaddressed. "He was just having a bad day," I told myself.

What the team and I did not know was that the company had lost a major partner that day, and the CEO received the news minutes before our meeting. The CEO was not in the right frame of mind to be giving feedback on our work. The right thing to do would have been to postpone the meeting.

The CEO's behaviour in the meeting dented the confidence of the team. As a consequence, the team second-guessed their professional opinions for months afterwards. Everyone was walking on eggshells when it came time to present work to the CEO, fearing that their designs did not "pop." The team suffered because I did not tell the CEO about the impact of his behaviour.

Back then, I had no framework for difficult conversations. I avoided them—to the detriment of my team. It took me a long time to prepare and find the right words. It took me even longer to understand the lasting impact of not addressing undesirable behaviour.

Then, I learned a framework for having difficult conversations. It now takes me less time to prepare for difficult conversations, and I am more motivated to have them. In this chapter, I'm going to share that framework with you.

Why are difficult conversations hard for quiet achievers?

I can think of three reasons.

Reason 1: It is a numbers game

For quiet achievers, social interactions are energy drainers. The more interactions we have, the less energy we have left. So the number of social interactions we have tends to be low—let us say four interactions on a busy day.

This means that even a single bad, difficult, or uncomfortable social interaction can have a drastic impact on our day. Saying no, for example, is usually a difficult conversation that leaves someone disappointed. If one of four interactions in your day is a difficult conversation like that, that's 25 percent—a whole quarter—of your interactions in a day.

Contrast that with an extrovert who is energised by social interactions. Let us say they have 20 interactions on a busy day. While a difficult conversation is still hard, it is only 5 percent—a small part—of that person's day.

So naturally, quiet achievers will avoid difficult conversations on a day-to-day basis: When they happen, they form a significant part of our day. And not only do difficult conversations drain our social energy, they also drain us emotionally.

In the long run, though, getting good at having difficult conversations is a numbers game. If your capacity for interactions is low to begin with, then you have less opportunities to practise regularly. To get good at difficult conversations, all you need is more opportunities to practise over time.

Reason 2: It is cultural

When I say culture, I mean the unspoken behaviours we accept (as a group) as normal without question. These behaviours can originate from the society we live in or the team or company we work within.

In some cultures, you never disagree with your boss in public. In others, speaking up equals participation, and participation is more important than being right; not participating means you are uninterested or disengaged. And in yet other cultures, you never say "no."

Our increasingly global and diverse workforce means more instances where friction between cultures might occur. For example, you might be part of a global company with employees based around the world working across global cultures, or a local company with employees around the world, or a team with neurodiverse team members.

Learning how to process our cultural differences, find ways to work better together, and handle difficult conversations with respect is key.

Reason 3: It is personal

I used to avoid difficult conversations because:

- I did not want to disappoint others or hurt their feelings

- I wanted to be liked and did not want to jeopardise my relationship with the person

- I was anxious and thought having a difficult conversation with my boss or superior was a career-limiting move

- I wanted to be a team-player and would rather "take one for the team" than say "no" and let the whole team down

Emotions are normal and part of being human. Learning how to manage our emotions is key to staying professional and doing the job we were paid to do.

Why can't I just avoid difficult conversations, sweep them under the carpet?

Not all jobs or occupations require working with other people. We can do a great many things on our own: Carpentry, baking, bookbinding, coding, painting, writing.

As individual creators, the only difficult conversations we need to handle are the ones we have in our minds with ourselves.

Difficult conversations in real life arise when we interact and need to work with other people. When we alone do not possess all the skills to bring our creation to life or to achieve the success we desire, it takes a team.

We cannot always choose the people we work with. And diverse teammates create friction points that need to be managed respectfully. We can hope that our teammates are easy to work with, but hope is not a strategy.

Working well with others takes work, and learning how to handle difficult conversations is part of that work.

If you are a people leader or manager...

It is even more important to speak up and have these difficult conversations in service of your team.

You are no longer just responsible for yourself; you are responsible for the people in the team you lead. If you do not speak up when you see bad behaviour, it sends a signal to your team that this bad behaviour is tolerated, maybe even accepted.

You might be thinking: *It is just one time. I will say something if it happens again.* Or: *I did not say something then, and now months have passed. I will bring it up at the person's next performance review.*

But, weeks or months later, you might wake up one morning and think:

- *I do not want to go to work today*

- *This team that I work with? I am not looking forward to seeing them. They are mean, and they fight all the time*

- *This is no longer a place or a team I want to work with; what happened? Where did it all go wrong?*

Choosing not to address bad behaviour is a slippery slope to even worse behaviour later on. Speak up in service of your team and show them where the boundaries for acceptable behaviour are.

Giving feedback is a good way to achieve this. Let me show you how.

Hard truths about giving feedback

Most people are terrible at giving feedback

Here's what usually happens when people try to give feedback:

- **The feedback is wishy-washy or unclear**: You are not sure what to do next, you are not sure if the feedback was positive or negative

- **"Shit sandwich"**: The people who deliver feedback try to hide negative feedback between two compliments—saying something good, then bad, then good again. It is clear as mud

- **It feels personal:** When giving negative feedback, it feels like they are criticising the person rather than the work

- **People do not give negative feedback**: They keep quiet and do not say anything, hoping that the issue will just go away

Feedback is not a gift; it is information

The saying "feedback is a gift" is bullshit. It asks us to accept feedback with thanks even when it is damaging, ill-intentioned, or just plain bad.

The truth is that most people are terrible at giving feedback. If you truly believe that feedback is a gift, then most people give terrible gifts.

I believe that feedback is just information—information that you can choose to accept or ignore. Feedback may be fact, or it may instead be someone's baseless opinion. Receiving feedback does not mean you have to accept or act upon it. What you do with the information is up to you.

The intent of feedback is to make the thing better

Try this reframe: The intent of feedback is to make the thing better. The 'thing' could be a piece of work, a process or way of working, a working relationship with another person, or a skill (helping the person level up).

The feedback you give is not directed at the person; the feedback you receive is not directed at you. It is directed at the thing.

By depersonalising feedback, you are less likely to take it to heart when you receive it and more likely to give feedback to others.

Remember: The intent of feedback is to make the thing better. Intentions are invisible. Hence, it is important to communicate your feedback clearly. The other person cannot act on the feedback if it is not clear or easy to understand.

Feedback framework

Giving and receiving hard feedback can elevate your emotional state. In these situations, having a clear framework helps you stay objective and on track.

Try this feedback framework:[8]

- **Situation**: When and where the thing happened; place, location, event

- **Behaviour**: What the person said or did. Not intention (intention is unknowable), not what you think the person thought—what was the behaviour that you observed, saw, heard?

- **Impact**: What effect did the person's behaviour have on you and/or the team? What did you feel? What happened to you and/or the team after the person's behaviour?

- **Consequence**: What lasting impact did the person's behaviour have or could have?

- **Change I'd like to see**: What is the new behaviour you would like to see from the person?

Here are a few examples of how it works.

Example 1:

(Situation)

Hey John. Last night…

(Behaviour)

…you left the toilet seat up.

(Impact)

When I went to the bathroom in the middle of the night, I nearly fell into the toilet…

(Consequence)

…and could have really hurt myself.

(Change I'd like to see)

Next time, can you put down the toilet seat after using it, please?

Example 2:

(Situation)

Hey John. At yesterday's team meeting…

(Behaviour)

…you interrupted me not once, but three times while I was in the middle of making my *one* point.

(Impact)

It made me feel as if what I had to say was not valuable…

(Consequence)

…and if this continues, I'll be less and less likely to speak up, even if I have something meaningful to say.

(Change I'd like to see)

Next time, can you wait till I'm finished before starting to speak, please?

Example 3:

(Situation)

Hey John. At yesterday's team meeting…

(Behaviour)

…you stepped in and made a decision on my behalf, even though it was a decision that was not urgent.

(Impact)

As Team Lead, I felt like a learning opportunity was taken away for me, an opportunity for me to make a decision I'd be responsible for.

(Consequence)

If this continues, I'm worried I'll be less likely to make decisions whenever you are in the room.

(Change I'd like to see)

Next time, can you defer and ask me what I think first, please?

Example 4:

(Situation)

Hey John. At yesterday's design critique…

(Behaviour)

…you told Jane that her design work "did not pop" and she should throw away what's been done so far and start again from scratch.

(Impact)

As VP of Engineering, your words carry a lot of weight, especially considering Jane is a less experienced designer who looks up to you. Frankly, even I would not know what to do next with your "did not pop" feedback.

(Consequence)

What you said really impacted Jane's confidence, and I now have to help her process and recover.

(Change I'd like to see)

Next time, if you don't like a piece of work but cannot articulate why, can you hold back and come to me first, please? I know how to give feedback that designers can action without damaging their confidence.

Sometimes, the behaviour is a symptom but not the root cause. Instead of prescribing the change you'd like to see, use this as an opportunity to dig deeper and find out what's really going on. Then, help the other person develop a change in behaviour that is acceptable to all parties. For example:

(Situation)

Hey John. At yesterday's team meeting…

(Behaviour)

…you rolled your eyes and waved your hand dismissively whenever Janet or Joseph spoke. This is the second time I've noticed you do it in two days.

(Impact)

It felt like you disagreed with them, but instead of voicing your thoughts respectfully, you chose a passive-aggressive way to show your frustration.

(Consequence)

As the leader of this team, I am accountable for the performance of this team. This behaviour of yours is one that I do not encourage and it has to stop now. If this behaviour continues, my next step will be to escalate it to your manager so that the three of us can discuss it.

(Dig deeper)

But before we go there, I wanted to discuss the frustrations you might be facing with Janet and Joseph. Can you tell me more?

Focus on the behaviour

When delivering feedback, focus on the behaviour: What did the person say or do? Use the five senses to guide you in identifying the behaviour to address. For example:

- **Sight**: Rolling their eyes every time a certain colleague speaks up, showing up more than 20 minutes late for a 30-minute meeting they were supposed to lead

- **Hearing**: Shouting at someone, laughing at them, saying out loud: "That is a dumb idea; who hired you?"

- **Touch**: Greeting a colleague by punching them hard on the shoulder

- **Smell**: Cycling to work and attending an in-person client meeting with unpleasant body odour

- **Taste**: Catering food for a company event but not considering the dietary needs of most employees

Behaviour is perceived. As the one giving feedback, you must witness the behaviour in action. Relying on gossip, hearsay, or a third party's account of what happened is possible, but tricky at best.

If you did not witness the behaviour, find evidence from two or three people who did witness the behaviour. And put yourself in a position to witness the behaviour next time.

Do not give feedback based on a person's intention

A person's intention is not perceivable. It is invisible. You cannot sense it. Do not give feedback on what you think they thought. Remember: You cannot read their minds (yet). You can never truly know what their intention is.

Always assume good intentions. Assuming bad intentions is a very slippery slope; you start imagining the worst in people. Your mind comes up with theories and stories that are not based on fact but fiction. Your judgement gets tainted and clouded; remaining objective becomes difficult.

In real life, assuming best intentions is easy to say but very hard to do. Imagine receiving feedback like: "Your work is terrible but I cannot tell you why; go fix it." How do you assume best intentions in others when you receive terrible feedback like this? We are human and we have feelings. It hurts.

I am here to tell you it is possible with practise. Here are a few tiny habits to help you stay objective.

What to do when you receive feedback you do not like

Do not respond to feedback while you are emotionally heightened. It is hard to remain objective. You might say the wrong words. And words, once said, cannot be taken back.

Imagine that a colleague said to you: "You have missed after-work social party drinks with the client three times in a row already. So what if you have a family and kids? You are letting the team down; you are not a team player."

In this scenario, you could respond: "Wow, I did not expect that. Thanks for letting me know. Can I think about what you said, and maybe we can discuss it tomorrow?"

Other times, a colleague might offer ideas or suggestions which sound like directives or instructions. For example, imagine that you are a designer and it is your job to design buttons on a webpage. Now imagine that a colleague says to you: "Make the button bigger! Make it red! Make it blink when you click it!"

As the designer, you know this is not a great idea. If you are calm and not in an emotionally-heightened state, and genuinely want to know more, you can say: "Ah! That's interesting. Can you tell me more? I'm curious: How do you think making the button bigger, red, and blinking will actually help the user? What problem will it solve for them?"

Sometimes, people give feedback like this because they believe giving *any* solution is being helpful—even if they are not the best people to be solving these problems. Sometimes, bosses do this without realising that their words and their seniority carry more weight than they know.

Your work relationship with this person is likely to be a long one. It might feel good to immediately respond emotionally, but it is more professional to respond after you have had time to process your emotions and thoughts. Remember: Words, once said, cannot be taken back.

Do not wait more than 24 hours to give feedback

If you give feedback too soon, you or the receiver might still be in an emotionally-heightened state of mind. This is not the best state to process or deliver feedback.

If you give feedback too late, the receiver might have forgotten what happened. Or you might make excuses not to give the feedback because it has been too long.

As a rule of thumb, do not wait more than 24 hours after the incident to give feedback. This will ensure sufficient time has passed since the incident for you and the receiver to successfully process your emotions and thoughts. At the same time, the incident will be recent enough that all parties will still remember what happened. The 24-hour timeframe also serves as a deadline so you do not sweep feedback you need to give under the carpet.

Preparing to give feedback

Use simple words. Minimise jargon. Be specific and concise. Choose the minimum number of words to communicate the maximum amount of meaning.

Write the feedback down; you may have to document it. Practise saying the feedback out loud. Picture yourself being in the room with the person. It will feel direct, and being direct can feel confrontational, but direct is clear.

Communicate empathy in your delivery with your tone of voice and choice of words. Refine and iterate your delivery till it sounds natural.

Give feedback in a 1:1 setting

There is saying which goes: When it is good news, shout it loudly from rooftops. When it is bad news, share it privately.

We can *guess* how the receiver will react to the feedback, but we can never really be *sure* if they will receive it well or poorly until we actually give the feedback.

When giving feedback, do it privately in a 1:1 setting. People are less defensive when no one else is watching. They are also more open to a conversation when no one else is listening.

Also use the feedback framework when receiving unclear feedback

Remember: Most people are terrible at giving feedback. If you receive feedback which is unclear, wishy-washy, or leaves you with more questions than answers, use the feedback framework to get clarity.

Maybe it was not clear:

- **(Situation)** When or where the thing happened?

- **(Behaviour)** What exactly you did to elicit this feedback?

- **(Impact)** How your behaviour affected people or things around you?

- **(Consequence)** If left unchecked and if you continued in your ways, what lasting impact your behaviour would have?

- **(Change they'd like to see)** What "acceptable" looks like? What needs to change?

Approach the conversation with curiosity. Difficult conversations can be hard for both the giver and the receiver.

Getting emotional is normal; it is human. Defer and step away if you are feeling emotionally heightened. The feedback framework gives you structure and will help you stay on course. Stay objective.

Tell teammates which areas you do (and do not) want feedback on

We work as a team when we cannot accomplish a task or project on our own. We need teammates to help us. Getting feedback on your work is part of working together collaboratively. But the worst thing you can do when asking for feedback is to let others give feedback on *anything*.

No one knows the context of your work better than you do. You understand the problem you are trying to solve, who you are solving it for, how you are measuring success, what constraints you are working within, the challenges you encountered when doing the work, etc.

Share this context before asking for feedback. Then, tell teammates which specific areas you want—and do not want—feedback on. This will help the team focus their attention on areas where you think their feedback will be most useful. It also helps you politely manage feedback that is outside the current area(s) of focus.

If all else fails, point out the risks and predict what will happen

There are moments when you find your team is moving in a direction that is against your judgement: Everyone has jumped onto the bandwagon heading, in your opinion, in the wrong direction.

You have tried for minutes, hours, days, maybe even weeks to steer the group and conversation toward the right course. Despite your best efforts, your teammates are not swayed or persuaded.

If the team chooses to continue down this path, try using this as an opportunity to point out the risks and to predict what will happen.

For example:

OK, it sounds like everyone is keen to launch with Option A instead of Option B.

However, I would not be doing my job if I did not highlight the following risks with Option A: Number one…

Number two…

Or

OK, it sounds like everyone is keen to launch with Option A instead of Option B.

So let me predict what will happen after we launch with Option A: Firstly…

Secondly…

If your predictions are right or if your risk assessment turns out to be true, you gain clout and earn respect from your teammates— maybe next time they will hear what you have to say. If you are wrong, this is a humble learning opportunity for you to realise that you may not have all the answers.

You cannot right every wrong, you cannot prevent every train wreck, and you will not always be right. Just do the best job you can in the time that you have, and let the chips fall where they may.

Chapter 7

How to say no (politely)

I travelled through Japan in 2019. While I was there, I observed that, whether it was at a 5-star spa resort in Hakone or a street side ramen stall in Kyoto, people almost never said "no" directly. Instead, they would offer alternative options.

This frustrated me at first: If the answer is "no," why not just tell me? I then learned that, in Japanese culture, saying "no" directly is considered impolite and rude.

In work contexts around the world, we do not say "no" for different reasons:

- We think saying "no" is a career-limiting move which may get us fired or impede a future promotion

- We say "yes" (even when we think *no*) because we want to be a team player and do not want to let the team down

- We want to be liked and do not want to jeopardise our relationship with the person

Consequently, we feel like pushovers. We feel bullied. We feel regret (*Why did I not speak up?*). We feel anger and resentment towards ourselves (*What is wrong with me?*) or the other person (*What is wrong with them?*).

What if the person is in a more senior position than me?

Power dynamics in organisational hierarchy are real: It is harder to say "no" to people who are above you in the company hierarchy.

A mistake I made early on in my career was to assume I needed to handle every situation on my own. I thought asking for help was a personal failure. I used to blame myself when I did not know how to push back or say "no" to unreasonable requests. I thought that I was weak. I thought that I was not working hard enough. I thought: *I will say no next time* (but I kept on saying "yes"). You might be experiencing similar things right now.

If you find the power dynamics in your situation exceedingly stacked against you, use your management chain. Speak to your boss. Hierarchies exist for a reason; one of them is to escalate issues that prevent you from doing your best work.

Your boss can:

- Coach you on how to handle the situation

- Speak to someone on your behalf

- Say no on your behalf

- Mediate a conversation with all parties to resolve the situation

Maybe it is your boss who you are finding it hard to say no to. Try the tiny habits in this chapter first. But if all else fails, even your boss has a boss who you can escalate issues to. And, for the most serious of organisational issues, you can escalate to your company's Human Resources or People and Culture Team. You do not need to do this alone.

But saying "no" is too hard. Why can't I just keep saying "yes"?

Imagine that there is a dark, hairy ball of negativity inside of you. It is dark and it is hairy. You do not like this ball, but it is a part of you. Most days, you manage to hide this dark, hairy ball in a corner of your mind. It is small and it doesn't take up too much space, so it is easy not to notice it.

The problem is, every time you say "yes" even though you think *no*, that ball of negativity grows. It grows bigger and bigger, and hairier and hairier, every time you feed it.

And one day, that ball gets so big, you cannot ignore it anymore. It is right there in front of you. It fills the room that is your mind.

It is there when you wake up in the morning. It is there when you go to sleep. It is there when you are sitting in a meeting. It is there the next time someone at the office asks you to do something you do not want to but you do not know how to say "no."

You cannot stand the people you work with anymore. You cannot imagine being there one more day. Most likely, you will end up quitting, even though you are good at your job and loved doing it in the beginning.

Sooner or later, whether you like it or not, a difficult conversation will happen.

Speaking up and actually saying "no" when you are thinking *no* serves you. The sooner, the better. Saying "no" keeps the dark, hairy ball of negativity from growing.

The overarching strategy of saying no (politely) is to make it a difficult "yes."

Let us say you are faced with the following scenario: Someone asks you to complete a task, but you have too much work and cannot take on any more new work.

Try the following tiny habits to say no (politely).

Ask questions, check for understanding

Approach with curiosity. For example:

Wow, this sounds really urgent. What happened?

Can you tell me more about this deadline? Is there a reason why it is so short?

Is the boss aware of this? What does she think?

Can I ask a clarifying question?

Let me reflect back what I heard to see if I got it right. You want me to…

Let me see if I heard you correctly. You want me to do this because…

Asking questions and checking for understanding helps the person clarify their own thinking as well: That urgent task might not be so urgent, that important task might not be so important, and that simple task might not be so simple.

Defer

Do not assume that you need to say "yes" or "no" immediately.

For example: "Wow this New Task sounds really important...Look, I'm happy to help...

(Ask about getting approval)

> ...I will need to get my boss's approval first though. I'm meeting my boss this afternoon. Can I let you know after?

(Ask for more time)

> ...Except something doesn't feel right and I'm not sure what it is. Can you give me time to think about it? I'll come back to you before end of today, OK?

Always give the person a deadline for when you will return with an answer. Set a deadline based on the importance and urgency of the task. Make sure the deadline is realistic—a deadline that you can meet.

If they insist on an answer now, the answer is "no."

Refer

You are not the solution to all things. You do not have the answer to every question. You cannot complete every task that is asked of you.

If you are not qualified, not skilled enough, or do not have the capacity for this new task, you can refer it to someone else. After all, doctors make referrals all the time.

For example: "Wow this New Task sounds really important...Look, I'm happy to help...

(Refer a qualified colleague)

...Have you met John in Engineering? He fixed a similar bug last week. I can introduce you if you want?

(Refer an available team)

...Team A actually just finished a big project and they are looking for their next one. Perhaps they can help with your task?

In such scenarios, you are not "passing the buck" to someone else. You are getting the person the help they need.

Re-prioritise

You can also ask the person requesting your help to assist you with re-prioritising your tasks. To do this:

1. Share current tasks/priorities

2. Set realistic expectations

3. Discuss new priorities

For example: "Wow this New Task sounds really important...Look, I'm happy to help...

> ...Right now these are my priorities: I have Task 1, Task 2, and this New Task. Realistically, I can complete two out of three by their respective deadlines. What do you think I should drop/give up?

Or

> ...I actually think Task 2 can wait, but Boss 2 will need to be OK with this. Let me speak to Boss 2 and get back to you, OK?

Do not use this tiny habit with a selfish, irresponsible bully who only cares that their task gets done. Only use this strategy with people who understand the importance of your tasks and the impact it would have if their task was prioritised over others.

Ask for something in return

If someone asks you for something over and above what is fair and reasonable, you can ask them for something back.

Asking for something fair and reasonable in return puts friction on their request. Suddenly, it is no longer effortless and free to ask you for something.

Think about it: If you are going to do the extra work, why should you not get something in return? Also, all work requires effort, so why should their request not require some effort on their part too? You can ask for more time, for them to get permission from your boss, for them to get a thing you need, and/or for extra time off.

For example: "Wow this New Task sounds really important...Look, I'm happy to help...

(Ask for more time)

> ...I'm going to need three extra days though. Can the deadline be pushed back?

(Ask them to get permission from your boss)

> ...If I drop Task 1, I can do this New Task. Boss 1 will need to be OK with this though. Can you speak to Boss 1, please?

(Ask them to get a thing you need)

> ...The only thing is, to do this well, I'll need our 2023 report. While I prepare, can you help get that 2023 report for me, please?

(Ask for extra time off)

> ...I will have to work over the weekend though. Can you organise two days off in lieu for me, please?

When making requests like these, refrain from using the word "but." "But" can trigger a negative response and put the other person on the defensive. Change how you phrase your sentences to avoid using the word "but."

Use a combination of tactics to say no (politely)

Combine these tiny habits for more impact. For example:

Ask questions + Re-prioritise + Ask for something in return:

(Ask questions)

Wow, this sounds really urgent. What happened?

(Re-prioritise)

I understand, but I already have Task 1 and Task 2 to complete before the end of today and I cannot take on another task. Which should I de-prioritise?

(Ask for something in return)

Can you check if the boss is OK with de-prioritising Task 2?

Re-prioritise + Defer:

(Re-prioritise)

> I actually think Task 2 can wait, but Boss 2 will need to be OK with this.

(Defer)

> Let me speak to Boss 2 and get back to you this afternoon, OK?

"No" is a complete sentence

Saying "no" is all about setting boundaries.

A boundary is a limit which defines where your work responsibilities start and end. Saying "no" lets others know where your boundaries are.

If you keep saying "yes," your boundaries get weaker and weaker. Soon, you will have no boundaries left, and people will walk all over you. Like a doormat. You are not a doormat.

Deep down, you know this already: If you keep saying "yes" (when you really think *no*), that dark, hairy ball of negativity inside of you will keep growing and growing. No one likes dark, hairy balls.

Saying "no" is hard, but saying "no" serves you. Saying "no" tells the world: This boundary is where I say—no more. You shall not pass.

You got this. If everything else fails, remember that "no" is a complete sentence.

Chapter 8

Networking

Networking is an activity that magically combines all the things that quiet achievers do not enjoy. And it usually happens like this:

You arrive in a room full of strangers. You grab a drink and stand awkwardly on the side, quietly scanning the room, hoping someone will make eye contact with you.

You see a group of popular people. They are laughing and deep in conversation, standing in a tight circle. You stand awkwardly nearby, listening, quietly laughing at one of their jokes (it wasn't even that funny), unsure of how to inject yourself into the conversation.

You see others just like you, scattered around the perimeter of the room, standing silently on their own with the same awkward look on their face, but you dread having to make small talk.

So you just stand there, drink in hand; you take out your phone and pretend to be busy. Deep down, you are wondering why you decided to come in the first place.

Sound familiar?

Networking does not come naturally to me. At events, I always feel awkward and nervous about meeting strangers. I used to find the nearest toilets and outdoor balconies—safe places where I could hide and escape the crowd for some quiet time. If alcohol was served, I'd drink too quickly, thinking it would offer me courage to do more extroverted things. Mostly, it just made me sick and I would end up sitting on the public bathroom floor, or I'd have to leave early so I didn't risk making a fool of myself.

Nonetheless, I knew networking was important. Over time, I developed these tiny habits to network authentically, online and in real life, in ways that suited me.

But I am awkward when meeting new people; why do I need to network?

Early on in my career, I struggled with the saying: "It is not what you know, it is who you know." I believed that being good at my craft was all that I needed to be successful. Meritocracy wins.

Then, there is another saying: "If a tree falls in a forest and no one is around to hear it, does it make a sound?" It made me think about writing the greatest book that no one reads. Designing the greatest app that no one uses. Making the greatest game that no one plays. Painting the greatest work of art that no one sees.

The thing about doing good work in the workplace is it actually takes two: One person to do the good work, and someone else to recognise that the work and the person are good. Most quiet achievers focus on the former, not the latter, because the latter requires people-ing.

For me, the goal of networking is resourcefulness—It is to grow the number of people I know who I can help and who can help me. Networking helps you meet good people who do good work, and for others to see the same in you too.

Networking, done well, connects you with interesting people and interesting conversations, and every now and then, interesting opportunities. Do not network only when you need a job.

What if I live and work in a country of people who do not speak my first language?

My partner's first language is French.

A funny thing happens when she is cooking and needs to split a recipe's quantities by half: She does the math out loud in French. "Trois cent soixante-quinze grammes divisé par deux..." ("375 grams divided by two..."). This is true even though she has spent most of her life living in countries where English is the first language. We think most clearly in our first language. We sometimes think in our native language first, then translate it to the local language when speaking up.

In my case, English is my first language. English is Australia's dominant language. Yet, when I first moved to Australia, I struggled to understand Australian phrases like:

- "How ya goin'?" (Meaning: "How are you?")

- "Good on ya!" (Meaning: "Well done, you!")

- "It is what it is" (Meaning: "This is a frustrating situation that cannot be changed and has to be accepted")

- "Bob's your uncle" (Meaning: "Something is easy to do")

I eventually learned these phrases, but in the meantime, despite knowing most of the same words, I still faced a language barrier. The important thing you have to realise is that *you* are not the issue—it is the language barrier. The good news is that language, like networking, is a skill—and skills can be learned and practised. Do not let language limit you. Just keep practising.

Networking feels very self-serving. How can I make networking feel less dirty and transactional?

Networking is all about making more dots so you can connect them later when you look backwards (a dot represents a new person you meet).

When making a new dot, focus on the dot you are making. Each dot is a gateway to new connections you could make in the future. You cannot connect the dots if you have no dots to begin with.

You should not try to connect the dots as you are making them. If you do, you will end up focusing all your energy on how this new dot can be beneficial to you or to other dots you know. This is bad because it means you are not present in the moment. You are not discovering the interesting and wonderful things that *this* dot is all about and has to offer on its own.

When networking, if you focus too much on how the dots connect, you lose sight of what makes *this* dot interesting in the first place. And you lose the ability to make more connections in the future.

Maybe this dot likes whisky or bookbinding. Maybe this dot was the first designer in their organisation to launch and scale their design system. Maybe this dot has five dogs rescued from the pound. Or maybe this dot travelled around

Mexico for two years during the Covid-19 lockdown because they could not get a flight home.

Sure, some dots will be more interesting than others. But even the most uninteresting dots could end up working at a company you really want to join in the future. Then, you have a connection you can rely on.

You may not know when you can connect the dots, or how the dots will connect. But the more dots you have, the more ways you could potentially connect the dots in the future. More is more.

Your brain works in weird and wonderful ways. If you combine that with diligently taking notes of new things you learned about your dot, you maximise the connections you can make in the future when looking backwards, and your new dot can do the same.

Networking doesn't just happen in real life

When people think about networking, they mostly think about events: Rooms full of new people you have never met, shaking hands and exchanging contact details. An extrovert's dream, a quiet achiever's nightmare.

This is simply one way to network; it is not the only way. It suits other people, but it's okay if it doesn't suit us.

Remember: Networking is all about making more dots so you can connect them later when you look backwards. You can make new dots in real life or online. Here are a few tiny habits for how to do it.

Networking in real life

Yes, I know. Networking in real life sucks. But if you have to, this is how you do it. Do it well enough and long enough, and one day, you might even enjoy it (once in a while).

Do your pre-work about attendees you would like to meet

Events like meetups and conferences usually have an RSVP list of attendees. Go through the list in advance and pick out people you would like to meet.

Look them up on social media and say hi. That way, when you meet up in real life, it feels less awkward, because you have already introduced yourself online. For example:

> Hi. I'm Jane. I saw that you work at Company A. I love your product. I noticed that you will be attending The Event too. I'd love to catch up. Maybe I will see you there?

Do not reach out to only one person. People sign up for events and do not show up more often than you think. Other times, your paths simply do not cross at the event. Having options maximises your opportunities to meet interesting people.

Walk the room

Do not just stand in one spot in the corner of the room. Meander around the room in a figure-eight pattern. This maximises your surface area and increases your chances of meeting someone interesting to talk to.

Walk slowly; do not sprint. Stick to a casual stroll. This is not a race. Your goal is not to be the first person to walk around the whole room. Your goal is also not to walk around the room more than everyone else. Your goal is to meet new, interesting people to have conversations with. Make more dots.

As you walk, scan the room and try to make eye contact with the people you pass by. Trust your instincts when sensing a connection. Stay open-minded.

Made eye contact but it feels weird? Smile, look elsewhere, and keep walking.

Made eye contact and it feels right? Smile, maintain eye contact, and walk towards the person.

Be ready to say a simple "hi" or "hello." Be ready with your pleasantries and small talk topics. Be ready to use your senses and respond accordingly.

See someone you want to talk to, but they are deep in conversation? Make a mental note, keep walking, and come back later. You do not have to hover. Hovering is needy. Do not be needy.

Resist the urge to look at your phone as an escape, unless you are looking up something about someone at the event. Remember: You are here to make more dots. Being on your phone makes it harder to use your senses or stay in the moment, and your body language will signal "don't talk to me." Connections also usually—though not always—begin with eye contact, and staring at your phone makes it difficult to make eye contact.

Join a queue

Events always have queues. There is a queue for food, a queue for drinks, a queue to sign in for the event, a queue for the bathroom.

A queue gives you a captive audience of two people to meet: One in front of you, and one behind. It is a liminal time and space as people wait for whatever they are queuing for to happen.

It is a great opportunity to make low-stakes small talk to pass the time and maybe make a new connection.

Don't like the people you are in the queue with? Leave the queue and join again. Queuing for food? Take less food so you can join the queue again shortly after and meet two more new people.

Networking online

In my opinion, social media is a gift from the quiet achiever gods. Before, networking in person was the main way to form new connections. But quiet achievers do not respond as well to networking in person as extroverts do.

With social media, we can reach across continents and across time zones, all on our own terms and from behind the safety of our screen. All of a sudden, all of the people we respect and want to connect with are right there at our fingertips. For me, a handful of deep, meaningful conversations means so much more than plenty of shallow, forgettable ones. And I'm sure many of you, if you're quiet achievers like me, feel the same.

Start meaningful conversations

Networking online is all about starting meaningful conversations with people you want to connect with. You can:

- Add a comment to someone's post about how much what they said agreed/disagreed with you

- Share someone's post and add your perspective

- Send an interesting post to someone who might find it interesting too

- Tag a person in a comment or post who might be interested in joining that conversation

- Create a post and tag people who you would like to start a discussion with

You can start and join multiple conversations at once, all with different people. Some connections take longer and require multiple interactions to form. Think of it like sowing many seeds when you only need a handful to sprout and grow. Start planting.

In time, an interesting conversation will spark an opportunity to take the next step and connect with the person 1:1. This can be via direct message or a short, scheduled video call. The cool kids call this "sliding into someone's DMs."[9]

Follow who they follow

People you find interesting will likely follow interesting people too. Check out the person's profile, and follow who they follow.

You are what you write, share, and post online

If these conversations happen in public channels, they represent your thought leadership. You are what you write, share, and post online; what you say and how you say it represents who you are.

The secret to speaking authentically is to not say things in private which you are not willing to say in public. Choose your words carefully.

Use a scheduling service to set a time to meet

Scheduling a time to meet a new connection over email or direct message could sound something like this:

Scheduling a time this way takes multiple messages and a lot of effort. You want scheduling a time to meet to be as easy and frictionless as possible.

Reduce the friction by using a free scheduling service like Calendly or Google Calendar. Invitees can select a time that suits them during timeslots available in your calendar.

You can say:

> Hi. I am looking forward to catching up. If it is easier, find a time slot that suits you on this link. Alternatively, give me two or three timeslots you are available and I will make one work. Speak soon! [Insert scheduling link]

If you are initiating a connection, choose your words carefully. Do not tell the person: "Please book a time on my scheduling link. Thanks!" This is presumptuous and puts the onus on the other person, not you, to figure out a time. Always offer an alternative that may suit your connection better.

You can also include a scheduling link in your email signature or profile description so people can self-serve and schedule a time to meet without the to-and-fro checking for availability.

Set up a regular cadence of catching up every two months

As you network, you will meet individuals you truly connect with and would like to talk to again. If you do not maintain these new connections, you will forget about catching up and the connection will go cold unintentionally.

Set up a regular cadence to catch up every two months. You can even set it up as a recurring meeting invite. At the end of your catchup, confirm when you are meeting again before you part ways.

Why catch up every two months? Because one month is typically too often and three months is too long. You need a sufficient amount of time to pass by for life moments to accumulate so you'll have new stories to share.

You do not have to do this with every new connection. Only the connections that are special to you. You decide.

Over time, some connections will deepen, maintain, and persist. Others will need a break; you have simply run out of things to talk about (for now). You will know a connection is waning when your catchups get postponed or cancelled last minute, or people do not show up for virtual meetings. Life happens, things get in the way, some connections falter and die a natural death. This is normal.

Assume best intentions and send a graceful message to reschedule. For example:

> Hi John. It was a shame we did not get to meet; I hope everything is OK. I've rescheduled our catchup to [insert date]; if that time is not suitable, you can find a time on my scheduling link: [insert scheduling link]. I was keen to get your advice on Topic A and how you would approach it. Speak next time!

Your perspective is always unique and always interesting

A limiting belief is a belief about yourself that restricts you in some way. Some common limiting beliefs about not sharing what you think online or starting meaningful conversations include:

- "I do not have enough experience. Maybe once I have worked longer in this industry, people will pay attention"

- "What I want to say has been said before by other people. It's not new"

- "This person is so important and busy. There is no way they would reply to something I said"

- "No one is going to listen to what I am going to say"

These beliefs limited me too. In 2018, I prepared a talk called "Design Leadership for Introverts." After applying to deliver this talk at multiple conferences—and after countless rejections—I finally got accepted in 2019. I was excited and terrified at the same time.

I had never delivered a talk at a conference before. I had never spoken in front of a large audience. I was worried that the audience would find my talk lame, fall asleep, or stand up and leave. I was afraid they would not get their money's worth. I was afraid of making a fool of myself. I was afraid I did not have the experience or clout for the audience to believe me.

Most of all, I was worried that everything I would share, the audience would already know.

Since then, I have delivered that same talk at several large conferences. I have also delivered the talk many times virtually. Every time, I've had audience members approach me after with thanks and appreciation:

- "Your talk really resonated with me. It was like you were in my head and you knew exactly what I was feeling"

- "I loved how practical your advice was. In fact, I'm going to try some out now at the conference!"

- "I always thought there was something wrong with me, but your talk made me realise that there are other people like me and I am not alone"

If you think I'm now free of limiting beliefs, you are wrong. I have never written a book before, and here I am writing a book—this very book you are reading right now. And when I was writing it, once again, my limiting beliefs appeared.

When was the last time you did something for the first time?

Doing something new always heightens our emotions and turns the volume of our inner critic up to eleven. Yet, it is only by doing new things that we accumulate experience.

Experience does not silence your inner critic and limiting beliefs; experience simply helps you recognise the patterns. Experience helps you recognise when you are held back by your limiting beliefs and gives you motivation to keep going, because you have been through a maze like this one before—and you are sure there is a path out.

If you are experiencing these limiting beliefs, hear this: Your perspective is always unique and always interesting. If what you have to say is true to you, if it is authentic and comes straight from the heart, you will have an audience, and your audience will feel seen.

There are people out there going through what you are going through. There are people out there who need to hear what you have to say. You just have to say it.

Networking online and in real life

Here are some tiny habits that work for networking both online and in real life.

Decide on a measurable output

When networking, have some measurable output. It might be exchanging contact details or adding the person on LinkedIn or X (formerly Twitter).

Remember: The goal is to become more resourceful by grow-ing the pool of people you know. You cannot do that if you do not know how to contact the person again when you need them.

After your conversation, record the following about your new contact:

1. Name and contact details

2. Where and when you met

3. Key points of the conversation you just had

4. (If you promised to follow up) A to-do list item

If you are networking in real life and have a business or name card, have it ready to exchange. I like writing the notes above on the backs of business cards I receive from contacts.

If you are networking in real life and want to connect digitally, the LinkedIn mobile app has a QR code feature. For someone to connect with you, they simply have to scan your QR code.

For example, this is my LinkedIn QR code. Scan it to follow me:

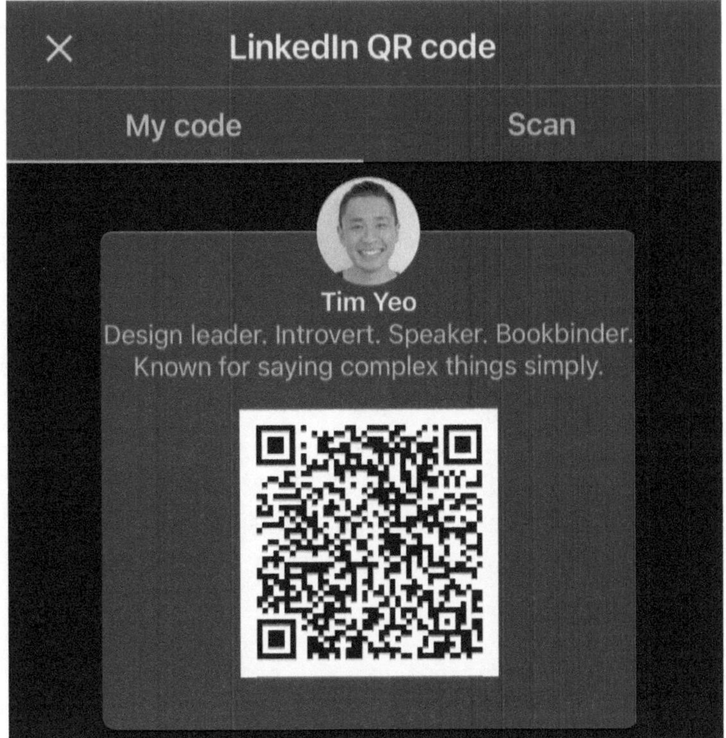

Follow Tim Yeo on LinkedIn

Ask to be introduced to two other people

So, you have made all this effort networking to get to know a person. In fact, you actually genuinely like this person; they are someone you can see yourself spending more time with.

Interesting people probably know other interesting people you should meet. So why stop at one?

When networking, do not stop at one. Ask your new connection to introduce you to two other people you should meet, and you can do the same for them.

Have an exit script

Sometimes conversations come to a natural end; we simply run out of things to talk about. What you must know is that this is totally normal.

Rather than having awkward silences, have an exit script ready so that you can leave and start another conversation with someone else (more interesting). Do this even when networking virtually.

Practise, practise, practise your exit script. Repeat it until it comes naturally. It could sound something like this:

> Hey John. I've really enjoyed chatting with you. If feels like we have a lot in common. Are there two interesting people you know who I should talk to? Can you introduce me? I'm happy to do the same.

Always be networking—methodically and consistently

We make excuses to avoid doing the things we do not enjoy. I know because I am the king of excuses.

If networking is hard for you, make it a point to always be networking—in small doses that you can manage.

If you do not enjoy networking in real life—but want to—set yourself a target of one. Just one. One in-person networking event every two to three months (the precise frequency is up to you).

Establish a networking cadence. In-person events tend to involve large groups of people and a lot of stimulation that will drain your energy. Rather than doing four networking events in one week and none for the rest of the year, do one networking event every three months. That way, you have time in-between to recover and deepen the connections you just formed.

If you are networking online, start or join interesting conversations for fifteen minutes every day. Add a comment to an ongoing conversation or share an interesting article or video while adding your thoughts and perspective.

Over time, your consistent efforts will add up and your network will get bigger and bigger. Remember: Tiny habits, done well, accumulated over time.

Chapter 9

For the ambiverts and extroverts reading this book

This chapter is for everyone who does not identify as quiet or introverted. Thank you for reading this far.

Most of the people I have coached are quiet and/or introverted—at least some of the time!—like me. But every now and then, others have approached me for a chat. Here is a sample of our conversations:

- "I've asked my introverted peer to 'just speak up more; it's easy. Here, I'll show you.' But it doesn't seem to work. Instead, they get quieter!"

- "I'm a new manager and I just inherited a team of people who are very, very quiet. Our meetings are like monologues where I am the only one speaking. How can I create a safe, inclusive environment so everyone on my team can thrive?"

- "They were so convincing when they were presenting their work to me 1:1. I worked so hard to get all the executives into a room to hear their brilliant idea, but as soon as I put them in a room with other people, they wilt! I just don't get it"

I have written this chapter because of one such conversation I had in 2023. I still remember our conversation like it was yesterday:

Jane was an extrovert, and she found herself on a team where the majority of her peers, bosses, and seniors were introverts.

Jane loved social interactions. She thrived on it. Whenever there was an opportunity to speak up, Jane did. It gave her energy. Saying words out loud was easy for Jane; it was how she processed her thinking. Speaking was cheap and transient; writing, on the other hand, felt final and much harder. Opportunity to present work? Yes, please! Brainstorming ideas? I'll go first! Jane's energy was boundless.

The problem was, Jane's team misread her intentions. They could not understand why she seemed to be seeking so much attention. Jane felt like a nail that stuck out. Her introverted bosses and peers gave her feedback like:

- "Why are you so noisy? Are you always this loud?"

- "If feels like you are seeking a lot of attention. Are you trying to show off?"

- "Why do you always have to shine and take the spotlight away from others?"

This did not help Jane. She could not be her full self at work. She became scared of speaking up, worried about saying the wrong thing unintentionally. Jane wanted to fit in, even if it meant having to pretend to be quieter.

Jane was constantly worried about what her teammates thought about her, which made it hard to focus on the work she was hired to do. All that chatter that she used to channel outwards, Jane turned internally unto herself. Jane was not happy.

Being ostracised, being misunderstood, being excluded is a feeling that I can identify with. As a quiet achiever living in a world where the extrovert ideal is desired, I could relate to what Jane was feeling, even though we presented as opposites.

Jane was different from her team, she did not feel like she belonged—so she pretended to be someone she was not.

No one should have to go through this. No one should be treated this way.

I remember telling Jane that sometimes it is not you, it is the place and the people that are around you that are not suitable. I remember sharing that intentions are invisible, but behaviours are observable—just because you talk out loud to process your thinking does not mean that your intention is to "steal the spotlight from others."

Jane later found a different job in a different place that appreciated her gifts. Jane did not need to pretend anymore.

Research says a third to half of the world's population is quiet or introverted in nature. That's a lot of quiet achievers. Learning to work better together helps all of us.

This chapter is for the ambiverts and extroverts who want to work better with the quiet ones like me. If you are a quiet achiever who works with ambiverts and extroverts, share this chapter with them if they want to learn how to work better with you.

Homogenous teams create homogenous ideas. Diverse teams create diverse ideas. Diversity can be our strength. Here are some tiny habits you can practise with the quiet achievers in your team so we can all work better together.

Share the agenda before the meeting

If you are organising a meeting, share the agenda before the meeting. This way, attendees can prepare beforehand. Coming to a meeting prepared is not just great for quiet achievers; it is great for everyone. All it takes is an extra minute before you click "send" on the meeting invite.

Not everyone will prepare beforehand, and that is OK. What you must know is quiet achievers are usually amazing at preparation. We like to ponder and process our thoughts until they are clearly formed in our minds before we share them.

This takes time, and we prefer to do our thinking outside of the spotlight of other people's attention. When you share the agenda before the meeting, we get to prepare beforehand. We get to do our thinking when we do our thinking best.

Offer to start a presentation or meeting

At a high-stakes meeting or a presentation with many attendees, offer to kick off the session before handing it over to your quiet colleague. Kicking off the session can include:

- Getting the attention of attendees so the session can finally begin

- Reviewing the agenda and why everyone is gathered here today

- Introducing the presenters

- Housekeeping (e.g. where the bathrooms are, what time tea break is)

If you start well, you are more likely to end well. Helping your quiet colleague kick off the session well will give them confidence to maintain that momentum and keep going strong.

Use a mix of silent and think-out-loud activities in meetings

We all process information differently. Some people think as they speak. Others, like me, tend to think more clearly in our minds before we speak out loud. Not all the time, but most of the time.

When a question is posed in a meeting and attendees are asked to respond, consider starting with a silent exercise: Everyone writes down what they want to say or what they are thinking before they speak.

This exercise only takes one to three minutes. Once that time is up and everyone is done, everyone can take turns sharing their views. If you have access to a collaborative documenta-tion tool (e.g. Confluence, Trello, Monday.com, Google Docs), all attendees can write down their thoughts publicly on the same document. Attendees can "show and tell" using the collaborative documentation tool as they speak, improving comprehension.

This silent exercise balances the playing field. The quiet ones have a few precious moments to process their thoughts in silence, while everyone else has a chance to practise with their inner voice before they speak. Win-win.

Give a heads up before you call on a quiet colleague to speak

Before calling on a quiet colleague to speak, give them a heads up. For example:

> Thank you all for coming on time. We are going to start with Topic A.

> Jane, I know you are an expert in this topic, and I will come to you in a few seconds to let you say a few words if you want.

> But first, let me go through some team updates.

By giving your quiet colleague a heads up, they are not put on the spot and immediately forced to think of something to say. Instead, they have a bit of time to process their thoughts before speaking up.

It might be a few seconds, it might be a few minutes—what is important is that you have signalled that it will be their turn to speak soon without putting the glare of the spotlight on them right away.

Allow for thinking time before expecting a reply

If you want a quality answer to your question, give quiet colleagues time to think beforehand instead of asking the question and expecting a reply on the spot.

Quiet achievers are amazing at preparation: We often need time to process our thinking before we share our thoughts. Quality improves when we have time to marinate on the question.

If you have a deadline, ask the question early and state a clear date and time by which you expect a reply. ASAP (as soon as possible) is not a deadline. A fuzzy question early is better than a sharp question late.

If you are expecting a discussion, tell us in advance so we come ready to contribute with talking points in hand.

Give them an "easy exit"

An easy exit is offering the person a graceful way to leave the conversation if they are not ready. You can offer an easy exit before you ask the question. For example:

> Jane, I'm keen to hear what you think. If you need a few more minutes, I can come back later, but I wanted to ask: What do you think of Topic A?

Or

> What do you think, John? It is OK if you need more time; I can come back to you later. But did you have any immediate thoughts?

Sometimes, you accidentally put your quiet colleague on the spot and end up watching them struggle to respond. You can break the uncomfortable moment by giving them an easy exit. For example:

> Do you need a few more minutes? I can come back to you later

Or

> Looks like you are not done yet. How about I go to Jane first?

By offering your quiet colleague an easy exit, they do not have to endure an awkward silence while being put on the spot. They also know they did not lose their turn to speak completely and can return to the conversation later, when they are ready.

Above all, the wrong thing to do is to not offer your quiet colleagues an opportunity to speak in the first place.

Use chat messages as the primary method for communication

On video calls, most participants rely on verbal communication as the primary way to communicate, just like in real life.

However, unlike real life, only one person can speak at a time on video calls. This can make it harder for quiet achievers to get their turn to speak.

You can level the playing field by accepting chat messages as a primary method of communication. Most video conference tools have a chat feature. Always open the chat window and read reactions, comments, and questions from the audience as the meeting progresses. If an attendee raises their hand, you can offer them the opportunity to speak after you are done talking. Tools like slido.com offer an anonymous, discreet way to ask and upvote questions. Share QR codes and links to ask questions early.

If no one on your team is doing this, start. Give attendees who raise their hand a chance to speak. Read out the messages you see in the chat. Lead the way and others will follow.

Ask your quiet colleague to help you read the room

Quiet achievers tend to be incredible listeners. Most of us are not in a hurry to speak up and share our point of view. We also tend to be amazing observers. We notice not just what people say, but also how people say it.

That means we tend to be better at reading the room: Noticing the subtle behaviour and non-verbal cues of people to get a sense of what they are thinking.

Reading the room can be hard when you are busy extro-vert-ing. So try having a quiet colleague be an extra pair of eyes and ears to help you read the room. For example:

- **(At the team meeting debrief)** You can ask your quiet colleague: "How do you think the team took the news? Jane spoke up and had concerns, but did you notice anything else from others who were quiet in the room?"

- **(As co-facilitators of a workshop)** Your quiet colleague might notice and say, "John, you looked like you were about to say something earlier. Did you want to share with the group?"

Small groups and 1:1 meetings can be more productive

Large meetings with many attendees are rife with tricky social dynamics. It is a competition just to be heard.

Such meetings tend to favour the loudest ideas, not the best ones; the attendees who are heard are just really good at getting the attention of others. Therefore, large meetings are not the most productive way to get things done.

Quiet colleagues tend to prefer 1:1s and are more likely to speak up in smaller group meetings of no more than five people. Make sure every attendee has an opportunity to speak up.

Offer to be a thinking partner

Most quiet achievers tend to do their best thinking alone first. However, we sometimes get stuck. We cannot get over a mental hurdle. We revisit the same pattern of ideas and spiral into a loop. We think ourselves into a mental corner and cannot find a way out of the maze. Some quiet achievers will have this happen more often than others, but we all have it happen sometimes.

In moments like this, offer to be a thinking partner. Play the role of sous-chef, collaborator, accomplice, running buddy. Be whatever type of thinking partner the quiet achiever needs. Your goal is to help clarify their thoughts or help figure out the best way forward. You are there for a short time, not a long time. Fly in, help, fly out.

Remember: It is not your thing, it is theirs. You are offering suggestions, not instructions. You are offering advice, not directives. You are not taking ownership, you are offering support. If you are their manager, be extra aware of the weight your words carry.

Do not be a seagull. A seagull is someone who flies in, shits all over the work, and flies out. The person who did the work is no better off; if they were stuck before, they are even more stuck now. They are left with the thing they made covered with seagull shit that they now have to clean up. Do not be a seagull. Help make them or their thing better.

How can you recognise when a quiet colleague is stuck? Here are some possible signs:

- They are obsessing over the one part they have a lot of experience in, but have not spent any time on the parts they have less experience in. You sense apprehension

- They are explaining all the many things they have made, but cannot explain how they all fit together. You sense anxiety

- When they explain the thing, it does not make much sense. You sense frustration or embarrassment

- They are quiet, really quiet, quieter than usual, and the more time passes, the quieter they get. The thing is not done, nowhere even close, and with each passing moment, the pressure to deliver gets heavier and heavier and heavier. You sense fear

How can you offer to be a thinking partner? Here are a few ways:

- **Offer at the start of the task**: "This task is complex and there are many moving parts. If you get stuck or are not making the progress you expect, let me know and we can chat, OK? Sooner is better. No question is too small; do not hesitate"

- **Ask for a signal**: "Hello! Just checking in to see how things are going. A simple thumbs up, thumbs down, or thumbs sideways will do. If you are stuck, happy to chat. If not, keep going and I will see you next week!"

- **Ask them to be your thinking partner first so they learn it is acceptable behaviour**: "Hey, can I get your help on this? I have been working on this design for two days now. It is almost there, but something is not right and I do not know what it is. I think I have been staring at this work for too long now. Have you got 20 minutes to help me think it through?"

When in doubt, offer to be a thinking partner sooner rather than later. The longer you wait, the more invested we get in our average ideas and/or the more awkward it gets to accept or ask for help.

As a thinking partner, you are there to listen and notice. Then, say what you notice, clarify things as needed, and offer suggestions (not instructions). This could also be a coaching moment or an opportunity to offer advice based on your experience. For example:

- **Notice:** "I noticed that all of the buttons are the same size, same colour, and same position on all the screens. Was that intentional?"

- **Clarify:** "Tell me more about this part again; I still do not fully understand it. Maybe try using different words this time?"; "Can you remind me: What is the problem you are trying to solve, again?"

- **Suggest:** "Have you considered doing Part Two before Part One?"; "What other options have you considered?"; "What did Jane think when you asked her for feedback?"

- **Coaching moment:** "What do you think is the real challenge here for you?"

- **Advice based on experience:** "I faced a similar problem before, and I struggled with it for a long time before I found a way to solve it. Would you like to hear more?"; "I have never faced a problem like this before, but when I have been stuck in the past, three things really helped me. Would you like to hear more?"

You are not going to be everyone's perfect thinking partner, and that is OK. If a thinking partnership is successful, offer to do it again. If it is not successful and the person is still stuck, suggest someone else they can talk to.

Ideas are delicate flowers. It takes courage to show unfinished work. Approach gently. Trust is earned with every passing conversation, paving the way for more honest conversations in the future.

Be our social butterfly: Join us at a networking event

Almost every extrovert I know has the gift of introducing people to each other. They can separate even the tightest circles at networking events to include others and make the circle just a little bigger.

If you find networking and meeting new people easy, bring a quiet colleague along for the ride. If a quiet colleague is unsure about going to the event, offer to go with them and never stray too far away.

If you are at an event and see quiet ones like us standing in the perimeter of the room, come and say hi. I promise, once we open up, our conversation will be very interesting.

Introduce us to others you know at the event. For example:

John you really have to meet Peter.

Peter, this is John. John has an Old English Sheepdog too! I mean, what are the chances; it is such a rare breed!

Chapter 10

Conclusion

Heaps of books and other literature that I have read about leadership, impact, and influence subscribe to the extrovert ideal. For a long time, I thought this was the only path.

Susan Cain's book *Quiet: The Power of Introverts in a World that Can't Stop Talking* showed me that a different path is possible. That there is more than one picture of what a leader and what success looks like.

Definitions shape you, but they can also limit you. So choose your definitions wisely. To close off this book, I want to leave you with the definitions of leadership and success that have shaped me.

What is a leader? A leader has followers. That is it. You can be a quiet achiever, you can be an extrovert—it does not matter. If you have followers, you are a leader. If you do not have followers, you are not a leader.

You do not have to be a leader to be successful. Leadership is a choice. Leadership allows you to have a strong say in the path and destiny of others. Leadership lets you steer a group of people towards a destination of your choosing. My desire to lead comes from the inside.

What is success? Success is leaving the world and the people you connect with better off than when you started. So long as you do that, you are successful. You can be a quiet achiever, you can be an extrovert—it does not matter.

My success did not come from singular moments of bravado. It came from practising every day, over and over, moment to moment. It came from tiny habits, done well, accumulated over time.

It is not an easy path. But it is a path I walk very comfortably in my own skin. I am no longer faking it, I am no longer pretending to be someone else. I no longer wear an extrovert mask. I stretched myself, I practised, and I kept the tiny habits that worked for me.

I am a quiet achiever who has impact and influence without pretending to be an extrovert.

I encourage you to do the same. Show up as the best version of yourself. Stop living someone else's version of success. Do your best work in the time that you have. And remember that work is work: Work is not you, and you are not your work.

You've got this. You are enough, and I wish you every success.

(Now go practise those tiny habits.)

I've finished reading the book; now what?

I wrote this book to be self-contained with everything you need to start making a change and having an impact at work. The key to your success now is practise.

The tiny habits in this book, whether public speaking or handling difficult conversations, are skills. Skills require practise to improve and maintain. Without practise, you lose your skills over time.

However, practising on your own is lonely, hard, and requires discipline. There is always something else more important to do, some chore your need to finish, some TV series you'd rather be watching. Sometimes, it is nice to have someone to practise along with you and to keep you accountable.

If you are done reading this book but do not want the journey to end here, you can do the following things:

1. **Join the Quiet Achiever Community.** Events, podcasts, articles, interviews with leaders you (probably) did not know were quiet achievers themselves. Meet and interact with other quiet achievers around the world. In the hundreds of coaching conversations I've had with quiet achievers, people often say: "I have no one else to talk to about 'these things.' You are not alone. You do not have to do this on your own. It is free to join.
members.thequietachievr.com/home

2. **The Quiet Leadership School.** The learning and practise continues online. The School's courses are for you if you need a structured, step-by-step guide on how to practise these tiny habits. Through video examples, I show you how to put every single tiny habit into practise. There is a course for every topic in the book, and more. You can binge-watch all the videos one after another, or you can skip around and watch a video on a tiny habit you want to practise right now. You choose how you want to learn. Every course contains exercises you can practise. Record a short video of yourself practising the tiny habit and post it in the course space. I will leave feedback on what works and how you can make it better. Plus, watch videos from other quiet achievers and be inspired by how they perform the same exercise in their own way.

   www.thequietachievr.com/school

3. **Coaching**. With 1:1 coaching, I'm your coach. This is for you if you need 1:1 help right now. It is personalised and customised for nobody else but you. Over live video calls, we talk through the challenges you are facing and what you want help with right now. I help you achieve your goals. Coaching requires chemistry, and I am not a good fit for everyone. But the quiet achievers I *can* help achieve their goals in days and weeks with my assistance—goals which would normally take them months or years to accomplish on their own.

   www.thequietachievr.com/coaching

4. **Tell others about this book.** Gift them a copy. Start conversations with other quiet achievers about the tiny habits you are practising and the difference they have made. Share the book with ambiverts and extroverts you work with so they understand what it feels like to be you. The more the world understands that being a quiet achiever is not a flaw, the sooner the world can leverage our quiet strengths as assets and work better together. Always remember: Tiny habits, done well, accumulated over time. www.thequietachievr.com/book

5. **Follow me on LinkedIn** and let me know what you think about the book. Scan the QR code below to follow.

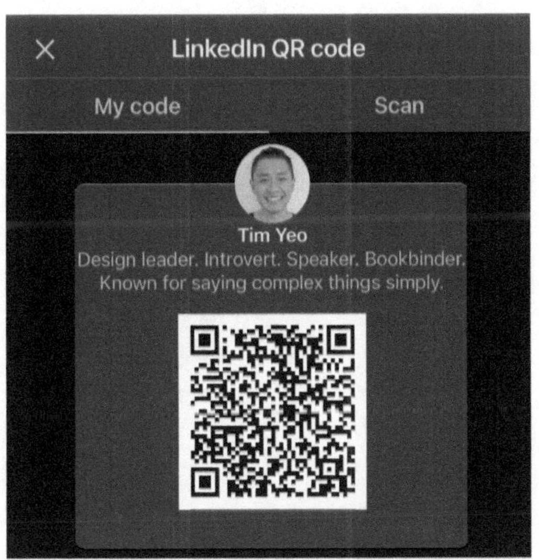

Acknowledgements

To the supporters who pre-ordered the first edition of this book: Thank you. Your support helped pay for the first edition copies, the editors, the book cover design etc. You supported this book purely on good faith. I hope I delivered. Thank you:

"Ahah" Lee Siew Hong, Irene Yeo, Eunbi Koh, Laura Wyatt, Teun van Olphen, Kara Jelley, Lois Teo, Evelyn Wijaya, Edwin Tan, Larry Cornett, Samantha Tan, Mark Patience, Stephen Cox, Gurdeep Singh, Timothy Greig, Holly Cole, James Leo, Simon Griffin, Tony Chng, Linda Nitschke, Lee Zejin Raemarie, Bryce Goh, Dominic Sebastian, Hang Wah Wan, Jeff Yeo, Megan Dell, Max Marele, Oszkar Nagy, Tony Tung, Jason Mesut, Jason Crane, Filip Szymczak, Chris Southcott, Joanne Ong, Susan Hansen, Chris Ellis, Farai Madzima, Thuan Nguyen, Louisa Ng, Phil Scott, Alysa Trinidad, Graham Dodds, Rachel Mah, Marcos Nähr, Damian Norton, Frances Yllana.

To my partner Angélique and my dog Bobbie: You fill my life with joy and love every day.

To my parents and family: Every day I thank you for raising me to be the person I am today.

Simon Griffin: The best boss I have ever had. I cherish your continued guidance, mentorship, and friendship.

Tomas Kopacki (TKO): Why you keep helping me, I have no idea. Thank you for generously giving your time to make The Quiet Achiever website real.

Natalie Soontornvinate: The best graphic designer I know. The book cover is stunning!

Ryan Rumsey and Larry Cornett: For sharing so generously your wisdom and your mistakes, having walked down this path before me.

Tutti Taygerly: For always creating a space for me to be heard.

Brian Hoadley: Thank you for your advice that pulled me out of the dark days of burnout.

To the consultant therapy group: Your fellowship, the laughs, the tears of our fortnightly chats make it easier to run a small business on my own. Thank you Mags Hanley, Samantha Soma, Bill DeRouchey, Erin Casali, Eva Schaforth, Billie Mandel, Holly Cole, Leigh Allen-Arredondo, Lisa deBettencourt, Steve Portigal, Noel Franus, Scott Berkun, Peter Merholz, Emily Parcell, and Ljuba Youngblom.

To John Allsopp of Web Directions, IxDA Milan 2020, Andy Budd of Leading Design Conference 2021, Jen Thomson of UCD Gathering and Steve Baty of UX Australia: Thank you for the opportunity to deliver my talk, "Design Leadership for Introverts," at your conferences. That talk birthed this book. You took a chance on a quiet person with no track record. I was nobody. You made me somebody. Thank you for taking a chance on me.

Dominic Sebastian and Megan Dell: Somehow you always find an angle of an idea I have never thought of. Thank you for being my muses.

Diane Tarshis: Thank you for your coaching and tough love.

Louisa Ng: My BB, my extroverted best friend.

Edwin Tan and Horace Tan: Brothers from other mothers.

Lois Teo and Stella Tan: Thank you for the memories and your candid feedback during the early days of the book.

To the early supporters of *The Quiet Achiever* in 2021. You supported the germ of an idea before we launched. Thank you Karen Ip, Shez, Yonnie Yeon, Pete Woodhouse, Matt Rose, Kaisen Wang, Lemon Mingyue Wang, Steve McKinney, Peter Fransen, Mary Nolan, Marsha Levina, Amy Zhu, Taryn Ewens, Julia Racsko, Azadeh Aghaei, Jeroen van der Ent, Sasha Annis, Jennifer Onyeagbako, Donna Lay, Molly Tilbrook, Dani Natividad, Alana Yick, Daria Kochuk, Agnes Lim, Stephen Cox, Eunbi Koh, Raemarie Lee, Madeleine van Dam, Scott Llewellyn, Ariff Razak, Lara Chen, Dawn Ta, Bethany Moran, Patricia Avila, Lois Baik, Lewis Ngugi,

Evena Rahn, Maigan Webster, Sophie Matrai, Leonardo Mattei, Iban Benzal, Rod Naber, Jackie Chang, Mateusz Kaczmarek, Jonathon Colman, Mags Hanley, Jason Mesut, Emily-Rose Hills, Hong Khai Seng, and Bob Baxley.

Lastly, to Susan Cain: Your Ted Talk and book, *Quiet*, helped me see my introversion as a strength for the first time in 2012. Thank you for making me feel seen.

Links, downloads, and additional content

Review the book

I hope you enjoyed the book and I'd appreciate a review:
www.thequietachievr.com/bookreviews

Gift the book to someone else

Know a quiet achiever who would benefit from reading this book? Send it to them as a gift:
www.thequietachievr.com/book#gift

Formats

When there is a book I really like, I buy the physical book, eBook, and audiobook. I dog-ear the physical copy, I listen to the audiobook when I'm mowing the lawn, and I read the eBook when I am in bed. The best book is the one that you have with you to read. If you'd like the book in a different format or an autographed physical book, get it from my website:
www.thequietachievr.com/book

Links and Downloads

- **Download a free chapter and a printable checklist of all the tiny habits in the book:**
www.thequietachievr.com/bookdownloads

- **Podcast**: www.thequietachievr.com/podcast

Backstory

The little QR codes scattered within the pages of this book lead to backstories. Scan the QR code below to view and listen to bonus content, or visit this webpage: www.thequietachievr.com/backstory

Notes

Chapter 1: Introduction

- [1] Susan Cain – Quiet: The power of introverts in a world that can't stop talking (2012) – ISBN: 978-0307352149

Chapter 2: Introducing yourself

- [2] Asynchronous vs Synchronous: What's the difference?
  https://www.dictionary.com/e/asynchronous-vs-synchronous

- [3] Rebecca Okamoto – Evoke – 5 ways to introduce yourself perfectly in 20 words or less https://evoke.pro/articles/238

Chapter 3: Small talk

- [4] Bruce Lee – Be like water
  https://www.youtube.com/watch?v=cJMwBwFj5nQ

- [5] Abraham H. Maslow – Hierarchy of Needs (1943) – "A theory of human motivation" – *Psychological Review* 50 (4): 370-396

Chapter 4: Meetings

- [6] Standup meetings – Wikipedia
  https://en.wikipedia.org/wiki/Stand-up_meeting

Chapter 5: Public speaking

- [7] Chris Cornell – Soundgarden: Superunknown – Black Hole Sun
  https://www.youtube.com/watch?v=ltc5EsuyBh4

Chapter 6: Handling difficult conversations

- [8] Taught to me by Paul Mills (https://www.paulmills.com.au) and an extension of the Situation-Behaviour-Impact (SBI) framework. https://www.ccl.org/articles/leading-effectively-articles/closing-the-gap-between-intent-vs-impact-sbii/

Chapter 8: Networking

- [9] Later Social Media Management – What does "sliding into the DMs" mean? https://later.com/social-media-glossary/sliding-into-dms

About the author

Tim Yeo is dedicated to empowering quiet achievers to make a big impact at work without pretending to be extroverts. With nearly 20 years of experience as a designer and leader in the tech industry, Tim has navigated environments dominated by big personalities with strong opinions and loud voices, gaining deep insight into the unique challenges and strengths of quiet achievers.

Since 2020, Tim has successfully coached hundreds of quiet achievers, helping them excel in various professional settings. His expertise includes mastering public speaking, handling difficult conversations, speaking up and performing in meetings, facilitating workshops, increasing your visibility in your organisation, saying no (politely), engaging in small talk without awkward silences, performing in interviews, and networking effectively online and in real life.

Best known for saying complex things simply, Tim is a sought-after keynote speaker at international conferences. When he's not coaching or speaking, Tim enjoys bookbinding and working remotely from his farm in Australia, where he lives with his partner and the fluffiest Old English Sheepdog ever.

Discover more about Tim and his work at **www.thequietachievr.com**

Follow him on LinkedIn: **www.linkedin.com/in/timyeo**

Book description

Do you squirm in your seat when asked to introduce yourself? Find networking awkward and embarrassing? In meetings, do you keep quiet even though you have something to say? Does your boss often tell you to "speak up more," but you're not sure how? Do you say "yes" to unreasonable requests, even though you want to say "no"?

If you answered yes to any of these questions, chances are you are a quiet achiever.

In a world that favours the extrovert ideal, quiet achievers often feel pressured to pretend to be someone they are not. Tim Yeo, a seasoned designer and leader in tech, lived this firsthand. For nearly 20 years, Tim tried to fit into an extroverted mould to succeed. It worked for a while, but left him feeling drained and inauthentic.

Tim wondered: *What's wrong with me? How do others make it look so easy? Maybe I'm just not good enough.* Determined to find a better way, Tim developed tiny habits to make an impact at work while staying true to his authentic self.

Since 2020, he has coached hundreds of quiet achievers to remarkable success. These quiet achievers now speak confidently in public, increase their visibility and feel more seen in their organisations, secure promotions, succeed in interviews, expand their networks, and engage in small talk without awkward silences.

Just because we are quiet does not mean we have nothing to say. In *The Quiet Achiever*, Tim Yeo shares the tiny habits he's used to manage his own introversion—practical techniques you can implement the very next day.

Discover how to harness your quiet strengths and thrive at work. Your journey to making a big impact while staying true to yourself starts here.

9 789819 402229